INSURRECTION:

Holding History

INSURRECTION:

Holding History

Robert O'Hara

Theatre Communications Group

Insurrection: Holding History is published by Theatre Communications Group, Inc., 355 Lexington Ave., New York, NY 10017-0217.

O'Hara, Robert, 1970–
Insurrection : holding history / Robert O'Hara. – 1st ed.
p. cm.
ISBN 1-55936-157-3 (pbk. : alk. paper)
1. Afro-American graduate students—Drama.
2. Slavery—Virginia—Insurrections, etc.—Drama. 3. Southampton Insurrection, 1831—Drama. 4. Grandfathers—United States—Drama.
5. Afro-Americans—History—Drama. 6. Time travel—Drama. I. Title.
PS3565.H296 I55 1998
812'.54—dc21   98-49485
                        CIP

Cover photo provided by the Library of Congress/CORBIS
Cover design by Susan Mitchell
Text design and composition by Lisa Govan

First Edition, February 1999

-- Preface

by Shelby Jiggetts-Tivony

Salman Rushdie wrote of Dorothy Gale, the heroine of *The Wizard of Oz*, ". . . what she embodies with the purity of an archetype is the human dream of *leaving*, a dream at least as powerful as its countervailing dream of roots. At the heart of *The Wizard of Oz* is the great tension between these two dreams."

Ronald Porter, the Black, gay protagonist of *Insurrection: Holding History*, estranges himself from his working-class, southern family by seeking the shelter and anonymity of an academic environment in New York City. Scholarship is not so much a passion as it is protection from the threats of AIDS, poverty, racism and ultimately, intimacy. Through the course of the play, Ron's desire to hold history evolves into the awareness that history is large enough to hold him.

I am excited by the publication of *Insurrection* for a number of reasons. First, to welcome Robert O'Hara, a young playwright whose own voice has been liberated by the bitingly satirical, profound and celebratory work of George C. Wolfe as well as the epic, exuberant intelligence of the plays of Tony Kushner. In *Insurrection*, the gay fantasia on national themes and the colored museum of Black stereotypes collide and merge.

Second, we now have another opportunity to gaze at that peculiar institution that enslaved millions and whose legacy enslaves many of us still. In *Insurrection*, we are reintroduced to Nat Turner, the prophet, preacher, and some say madman and murderer, whose rebellion is still the stuff of historical and literary revisionism. To invoke one of the most blood-drenched chapters in a people's struggle for freedom and add a "FULL-THROTTLE, NO-HOLDS-BARRED, 11:00, BROADWAY, SHOWSTOPPING, BRING DOWN THE HOUSE, PRODUCTION NUMBER, Chains and all" takes the kind of bodaciousness that is as liberating as it is initially shocking. But to know that we move toward a twenty-first-century American theatre with so much gumption and our collective sense of humor intact is a joy and a relief.

Finally, I just love this play! I know that my former colleagues at The Joseph Papp Public Theater/New York Shakespeare Festival share both my pleasure at being a part of its development and my hope that this is the first of many fine plays to come from Mr. O'Hara.

As the character Ron reconciles his need to leave with a deeper understanding of the roots that will forever ground and nourish him, we can collectively share the pain and catharsis of holding history.

Shelby Jiggetts-Tivony
Dramaturg, *Insurrection: Holding History*
The Joseph Papp Public Theater/New York Shakespeare Festival
December 1998

Acknowledgments

during the early part of 1994 as i sat in my bed after having my dead grandfather visit me in my dreams this play began to form itself. in that dream my grandfather, T.J. nicknamed Judge, whispered 3 words to me, "take. me. home."

the following **acknowledgments** are for those who helped bring that dream to reality:

my mother, Lillie Ann, my grandmother Lizzie Bee and the rest of the O'Hara Family gave me a childhood so rich and insane that my imagination lives on in Overdrive.

the Cast and Crew of my MFA Thesis production, Richarda, Karamu, David, Duane, Heather (my wife), Edward, Benja, Spencer, Messeret, Nella, Tracey, Kaye, Colin, and Doey were there from the beginning making their way in the cold to a small dark basement in harlem every day for 4 weeks for no money no fame no glory but simply the love of the Theater. they are still my Foundation and Friends Forever.

George C. Wolfe, mentor and taskmaster, forced my Art and my Self to grow in leaps and bounds and provided me with my 1st. Artistic Home.

my 2nd Family at the Public including Rosemarie, Shirley, John, Carol, Brian, Tom, Donna and many many others on Lafayette Street made the World Premiere possible.

Carey Perloff and my 3rd Family at ACT treated me like a king and provided me a room and stage to "let my spirits SPEAK."

Gordon Davidson, Robert Egan, Oliver Mayer and the staff of the Mark Taper Forum helped an infant of a writer to grow feet and develop this play before any one else.

Charles Randolph-Wright and Timothy Douglas each brought a fierceness of talent and love of language to their productions which allowed me to SEE. safe in the thought that there was Something in the words i'd written.

Shelby Jiggetts-Tivony asked the difficult questions and gave me that much needed encouragement to push further and see the light at the end of the tunnel. the american theater needs you shelby, come back baby come back!

my professors and fellow students at Columbia University were committed to developing the Artist inside me.

the National Endowment for the Arts, Theatre Communications Group, Audrey Skirball-Kenis Theater Projects, the Sherwood Family and *Newsday* provided me with additional financial stability during the development of this play.

Prof. Doc Collins was the first to look me in the eye and say, "rob, you're a writer . . ." i love you Doc.

Insurrection: Holding History is dedicated to the Memory of my Grandfather, T.J. O'Hara. as i grow older i wish even more that he were still here but i continue to Hold His Story as he Holds Mine.

INSURRECTION:
Holding History

the 4 productions below made this play what it is today.

Insurrection: Holding History was first performed in an Actor's Equity Association-approved Showcase production presented by The Oscar Hammerstein II Center for Theater Studies, School of the Arts, Columbia University, as Robert O'Hara's MFA Directing Thesis, April 1995. it was directed by Robert O'Hara. sets were designed by Doey Luethi, costumes by Kaye Voyce, lights by Colin D. Young. the dramaturg was Liz Engelman, general manager was Nella Vera and the stage manager was Tracey Mitchel.

the acting ensemble was as follows:

MUTHA WIT/MUTHA	Richarda Abrams
T.J.	Karamu Kush
NAT TURNER/OVA SEEA JONES	David Larrick Smith
RON	Duane Boutté
OCTAVIA/KATIE LYNN	Heather Simms
GERTHA/CLERK WIFE/MISTRESS MO'TEL	Benja Kay
REPORTER/COP/CLERK HUSBAND/	
BUCK NAKED/DETECTIVE	Edward Nattenberg
HAMMET	Spencer Barros
CLERK SON/IZZIE MAE	Messeret

a Workshop production presented by Center Theater Group/ Mark Taper Forum as part of their New Work Festival, December 1995. it was directed by Timothy Douglas. set consultant was Rachel Hauck, costume consultant was Maggie Morgan, lighting consultant was Michael Nevitt.

the acting ensemble was as follows:

MUTHA WIT/MUTHA	Juanita Jennings
T.J.	Gregory Wallace
NAT TURNER/OVA SEEA JONES	Ellis E. Williams
RON	Demitri Corbin
OCTAVIA/KATIE LYNN	Kimberleigh Aarn
GERTHA/CLERK WIFE/MISTRESS MO'TEL	Cleo King
REPORTER/COP/CLERK HUSBAND/	
BUCK NAKED/DETECTIVE	Edward Nattenberg
HAMMET	Robert Barry Fleming
CLERK SON/IZZIE MAE/SHERIFF	Regina Byrd Smith

the World Premiere was presented by The Joseph Papp Public
Theater/New York Shakespeare Festival, George C. Wolfe,
Producer, November 1996. it was directed by Robert O'Hara.
sets were designed by James Schuette, costumes by Toni-Leslie
James, lights by David Weiner, sound by Red Ramona, music
composed by Zane Mark, choreographed by Ken Roberson,
production dramaturg was Shelby Jiggetts-Tivony.

the acting ensemble was as follows:

MUTHA WIT/MUTHA	Vickilyn Reynolds
T.J.	Nathan Hinton
NAT TURNER/OVA SEEA JONES	Bruce Beatty
RON	Robert Barry Fleming
OCTAVIA/KATIE LYNN	Heather Simms
GERTHA/CLERK WIFE/MISTRESS MO'TEL	Ellen Cleghorne
REPORTER/COP/CLERK HUSBAND/	
BUCK NAKED/DETECTIVE	T.J. Kenneally
HAMMET	Jeremiah W. Birkett
CLERK SON/IZZIE MAE	Sybyl Walker

the West Coast Premiere was presented by the American Conservatory Theater, January 1998. it was directed by Charles Randolph-Wright. the sets were designed by Yael Pardess, costumes by Beaver Bauer, lights by Peter Maradudin, music by Edwin Hawkins, sound by Garth Hemphill.

the acting ensemble was as follows:

MUTHA WIT/MUTHA	Velina Brown
T.J.	L. Peter Callender
NAT TURNER/OVA SEEA JONES	Steven Anthony Jones
RON	Gregory Wallace
OCTAVIA/KATIE LYNN	Anika Noni Rose
GERTHA/CLERK WIFE/MISTRESS MO'TEL	Shona Tucker
REPORTER/COP/CLERK HUSBAND/	
BUCK NAKED/DETECTIVE	Marco Barricelli
HAMMET	Raphael Peacock
CLERK SON/IZZIE MAE	June A. Lomena

The Characters

8 Negros n' 1 Cracker
Play All of the Following
   Characters:

Ron
T.J.
Mutha Wit/Mutha
Gertha/Clerk Wife/Mistress Mo'tel
Octavia/Katie Lynn
Nat Turner/Ova Seea Jones
Clerk Son/Izzie Mae
Reporter/Cop/Clerk Husband/Buck Naked/Detective
Hammet
and Random Field Slaves

Time

Now and Then

Place

Here and There

Note

All lines and actions denoted with an * should be performed
simultaneously

this play should be done as if it were a Bullet through Time

A BACKYARD
RON READS a version of THE CONFESSIONS OF NAT
TURNER.
next to RON is
T.J. who is the GREAT-GREAT-GRANDFATHER, who is the SHINER,
who is the 189-year-old man, who has inhabited a wheelchair for the
last 100 years, who can move nothing on his body EXCEPT his left
eye and the middle toe of his right foot
there is a THUD
it comes from OFFSTAGE
there is another
THUD
it is the bass line of music playing off
THUD
beat.
RON lifts a Pencil and makes a note in the BOOK
as he writes
FAMILY & FRIENDS *(Offstage):* the ROOF the ROOF the
    ROOF IS ON FIRE!!!!!
        (Ron's Pencil breaks
        he looks toward
        THUD
        he sighs
        he rolls his eyes
        he looks to T.J.
        silence.
        then
        THUD

he grabs his BOOKbag
inside is a portable CD player
THUD
he finds the CD his special CD placing it inside the player plac-
    ing the headphones on his Head
THUD
as the CD plays
we hear
MUTHA WIT who is the ROOT, who gives voice to T.J.
she SINGS a lullaby
for RON
the CD drowns out the
THUD
but.
he feels something. different.
a
presence.
he removes his Headphones
he looks to T.J.
AS MUTHA WIT APPEARS
he doesn't see HER
he feels HER
RON listens to MUTHA WIT.
he allows her to
enter
she moves
closer
inside.
RON sees
NAT TURNER who is the INSURRECTIONIST, who is the
    SLAVE, who is the PROPHET, who is the HATCHET
    MURDERER; NAT FLEES into the dark safety of the
    woods.
RON starts to follow NAT
but there
right
there

HAMMET appears.
HAMMET who is NAT TURNER's right-hand man, who is the
other SLAVE, who is a walking Beauty; HAMMET
SEARCHES for NAT TURNER.
HAMMET stops he sees RON.
RON stops he sees HAMMET.
his Breath is taken away
a WHITE REPORTER enters the BackYard and approaches
RON.
instantly
HAMMET escapes.
* *not noticing the REPORTER, slowly RON goes back to the*
BOOK and T.J.)

* FAMILY & FRIENDS *(Offstage)*: WORK OCTAVIA WORK.
WORK THOSE BRAIDS. HEY!! WORK OCTAVIA
WORK. WORK THOSE BRAIDS. HEY!! SIDE TA SIDE.
UP N' DOWN. SIDE TA SIDE. UP N' DOWN. WORK
GERTHA WORK. WORK GERTHA WORK. SHAKE IT
MAKE SHO YOU DON'T BREAK IT SHAKE IT MAKE
SHO YOU DON'T BREAK IT. FISHTAIL. FISHTAIL.
FISHTAIL. HEY. WORK THAT CRACK BABY. WORK
THAT CRACK MAMA. WORK THAT CRACK DADDY.
(Deep-voiced) THE CRACK FAMILY. THE CRACK FAMI-
LY HEY. ROACHES. ROACHES. ROACHES ON THE
WALL-ALL WE DON'T NEED NO RAID LET THE
MUTHERFUCKAS CRAWL-ALL. HEY PARTY OVA
HEAH. PARTY OVA HEAH. PARTY OVA HEAH.
OWWWW . . .

REPORTER: how does it feel to know that your Great-Great-
Grandfather is still alive after all this time?

RON *(Laughing)*: you know, every year you never fail to ask the
same questions. i mean . . . it feels good.

REPORTER: What about the reports that the Government
wants to do some tests on Mr. T.J. to figure out if he's
actually alive or just some dummy that you all got rigged
up to get publicity every year?

RON *(Final)*: . . . my grandfather is in wonderful health for a 189-year-old man

REPORTER: has he moved yet

RON: as you well know he can only move his left eye and his middle toe on his right foot.

REPORTER: how do you all know that Mr. T.J. is actually 189 years old and that his birthday is actually today I mean did any slave really know his date of birth in Africa didn't they go by the moons or something?

(beat.)

RON: he told me.

REPORTER: but isn't it true he hasn't spoken in this century?

RON: he shines.

REPORTER: could you explain what you mean when you say mr. T.J. "shines"? is there any voodoo involved here?

RON: heah you go wit yo' voodoo shit again
i don't mean ta be rude o' nuthin but—

FAMILY & FRIENDS *(Offstage)*: IF YOU DON'T IF YOU DON'T IF YOU FUCK YOU IF YOU DON'T IF YOU DON'T WANNA PARTY TAKE YO' BLACK ASS HOME!!! *(2X)*

(another VISION appears of
NAT TURNER racing through the woods
TURNER huffs. He puffs.)

* HEY!! RUFF-RUFF RUFF-RUFF BOW-WOW BOW-WOW RUFF-RUFF RUFF-RUFF BOW-WOW BOW-WOW . . .

(* NAT is frightened out of the woods by the BARKING.
HE surrenders himself to a JAIL CELL.
TURNER SUFFERS.
HE PRAYS.
RON turns to T.J.

HAMMET reappears Deep in the Woods
Watching
AS
The REPORTER, desperate for a story, now sees and crosses to
TURNER.)

REPORTER: Mr. Turner?

(No Answer.)

Mr. Nat Turner? . . . My name is Thomas R. Gray and I'm
here to take your confession.

(No Answer.)

Mr. Turner? . . .

(No Answer.)

Look you can give me your story or I can make it up and
even if you do confess to me I'm probably gonna put in
a little filler here and there so listen Nigga yo' silence
will do you no benefit you dig? because these country
white folks ain't gonna let you breathe much longer
after going out here with a hatchet and chopping up
every white face you could find.

(No Answer.
RON and HAMMET Watch. Stunned. AS:
The REPORTER begins to WRITE.)

. . . the CONFESSIONS of NAT TURNER . . .
the leader of the late insurrection in Southampton
Virginia as fully and voluntarily—
NAT: . . . Blood on the Corn . . .
REPORTER: That's better SPEAK.
NAT: . . . The Sun turned Black . . .

REPORTER: SPEAK and Books about Books about you will be
    written.
NAT: . . . Figures Hieroglyphics Numbers . . .
REPORTER: SPEAK. and history shall REVERBERATE with
    your name.
NAT: My name is
    Nat. Turner.

(*A Police HELICOPTER Appears above and Drowns TURNER
in Light.
FAMILY and FRIENDS Appear in BackYard
the following cacophony of sound envelopes RON and HAM-
MET.*)

* FAMILY & FRIENDS: FISHTAIL. FISHTAIL. FISHTAIL.
        HEY!!
    SPEAK.
    THE CRACK FAMILY! THE CRACK FAMILY! HEY!!
    SPEAK.
    ROACHES, ROACHES, ROACHES IS ON THE WALL
    SPEAK.
    SHAKE IT MAKE SHO YOU DON' BREAK IT
    SPEAK.
    SIDE TA SIDE UP N' DOWN SIDE TA SIDE UP N'
        DOWN
    SPEAK.
    BOW-WOW BOW-WOW
    WORK NAT WORK!
    WORK PROPHET WORK!
    WORK NAT WORK!
* NAT: And a Voice said unta me—
    SUCH IS YOUR LUCK SUCH YOU ARE CALLED TO
        SEE
    LET IT COME ROUGH OR SMOOTH YOU MUST
        BEAR IT ALL.
    The ALMIGHTY whispered to me
    The HOLY GHOST sang

FIGHT AGAINST THE SERPENT
BLACK AND WHITE SPIRITS IN BATTLE.
THE BLOOD OF CHRIST WAS ON THE CORN
cos that DAY was fast approaching—
when the FIRST should be LAST
and the LAST should be FIRST
FIRST. LAST. LAST. FIRST.
FIRST. LAST. LAST. FIRST.
FIRST. LAST. LAST. FIRST.
(weak) first.—last—last—first.

* REPORTER *(A live broadcast)*: What do you think the DNA
tests on your Blood samples found in the cornfields will
prove Mr. Turner and is it true your semen was found in
the mouth and ears of several of the white children that
you murdered? What about reports that all three major
networks and TURNER NETWORK TELEVISION
which many feel is owned by the distant relative of your
former now decapitated slave master what about
reports that they all offered you 6 figure deals for your
story and film rights? who do you think should portray
you in the 8 hour mini-series that FOX TELEVISION
wants to produce? many blacks have called you their
HERO Mr. Turner any thoughts on that?

Dead. white men white women white babies amount-
ing to 55. Dead.

(SILENCE.)

The judgement of the court is that
you be taken hence to the jail from whence you came
thence to the place of execution and
on Friday next between
the hours of 10am and 2pm
FAMILY & FRIENDS: work prophet work
REPORTER: be hung by the neck until you are
NAT: FIRST.
REPORTER: DEAD.

NAT: LAST.

REPORTER: DEAD.

NAT: LAST.

REPORTER: DEAD.

NAT: FIRST.

REPORTER: and may the lord have mercy upon your soul.

FAMILY & FRIENDS: IF YOU DON'T IF YOU DON'T IF YOU
FUCK YOU IF YOU DON'T IF YOU DON'T WANNA
PARTY TAKE YO' BLACK ASS HOME.

—————————————————— A Midnight Shine

RON massages T.J.'s left eye and the middle toe on his right foot.
note. MUTHA WIT Speaks for T.J. until otherwise noted.
pause

RON: . . . how ya feelin'?

MUTHA WIT: Old.

RON: Like your party?

MUTHA WIT: Borin'.

RON: Huh?

MUTHA WIT: Borin' people borin' party.

RON: . . . how that feel gramps?

MUTHA WIT: Mo' eye.

RON: It's late. i gotta go back to new york tonight you know.

MUTHA WIT: Ain't you don' wit that yet?

RON: I just gotta finish my thesis

MUTHA WIT: What's a thesis?

RON: it's a long paper I gotta write

MUTHA WIT: Then what you do after you don' wrote it?

RON: Then I gotta show it to a bunch of white folks.

MUTHA WIT: Then what?

RON: Hopefully I can get paid like one of them white folks.

MUTHA WIT: Then what?

RON: . . . Gramps . . .

MUTHA WIT: Then what?

RON: Then nuthin. What you mean then what? Then I'm done. I git a job. I live, become fabulously rich and mildly famous.

MUTHA WIT: Then what?

RON: Then I drop dead I guess I don't know.

MUTHA WIT: I didn't.

RON: You didn't what?

MUTHA WIT: Drop dead.

(OCTAVIA appears in front of her bedroom mirror, feeling her body.
After a moment, GERTHA enters.)

GERTHA: What you doing?

OCTAVIA: Mama take a look at my boobies.

GERTHA: What about 'em?

OCTAVIA: Take a good look at 'em.

GERTHA: What?

OCTAVIA: Don't this left one look a lot longer than the otha one?

GERTHA: octavia are you pregnant?

OCTAVIA: naw mama i ain't pregnant what you talkin' look at my lips nah don't the bottom look a li'l bigger than the top?

GERTHA: go'n to bed octavia i told you ta lay offa that punch.

OCTAVIA: mama i'm serious come look at somethin' nah don't my butt look bigga to you?

GERTHA: you always had a big butt

OCTAVIA: no you the one always had the big butt don't even try it.

(GERTHA and OCTAVIA Go to RON.)

GERTHA: Ronnie why ain't you don' put 'im in bed?

RON: we was just going he wanted to have a man to man talk.

OCTAVIA: With who?

RON: Funny.

GERTHA: you barely spoke tonight head buried in that book you ack lak you too good ta com' hang wit the heathens

RON: it's not that Aint Gertha

GERTHA: thems yo' peoples there tonight don't neva git too high on readin' and writin' you can't bump and grind wit' yo' folk

RON: i know i'm sorry i'm um . . . a little preoccupied . . .

GERTHA: you really gotta go back this late? you can't stick around for none of your aint gertha's home cookin'?

RON: no aint gertha i have a very important meeting to prepare for.

OCTAVIA: let him go git his edu-ma-cation, i'll eat yo' home cookin' mommy.

(GERTHA looks Octavia up and down, focusing on her belly.)

GERTHA: ronnie i think your cousin octavia heah must think you got a fool fo' a Aunt she must think i ain't gat no eyes ta see nuthin.

RON *(Quick)*: octavia i know you ain't sittin' up in heah pregnant?

*(OCTAVIA snaps her lips and rolls her eyes.
RON and GERTHA look at each other.)*

GERTHA & RON: hmmp.

GERTHA: . . . his p.j.s out on the bed Nite Gramps Happy Birthday.

OCTAVIA: Nite Old Man!!

GERTHA: Octavia gul!?!

OCTAVIA: I just wanted to see if he'd move. he probably cain't even hear us he probably thought we was a bunch of crazy baboons this evenin' hoopin' and hollerin' didn't ya gramps? you done gone deaf too ain't ya gramps?

GERTHA: Don't talk lak that 'bout yo' Gramps this man useta be a slave.

OCTAVIA: And?

GERTHA: And that means somethin'.

OCTAVIA: What?

GERTHA: That you ain't suppose ta talk 'bout 'im that's what now shut up heifa and say goodnite lak a decent human person.

OCTAVIA: nite gramps. happy birthday.

GERTHA: that's better. ronnie i left a li'l somethin' in the kitchen fo' yo' plane ride you have a safe trip baby.

RON: thank you Aint Gertha.

(GERTHA Exits.)

OCTAVIA: nite head. i'm comin' up to visit that school next month remember.

RON: you gotta keep yo' grades up to get into my school

OCTAVIA: you ain't gatta tell me that . . .
(smile) i gats plans.

(OCTAVIA Sashays Out.)

MUTHA WIT: ya brain busy boy

RON: what?

MUTHA WIT: ya brain busy

RON *(Tired)*: . . . this thesis is kickin' my ass gramps

MUTHA WIT *(Quick)*: watch ya mouth

RON: sorry.
it's just, i gotta have an outline on the dean's desk by Monday afternoon or

MUTHA WIT: or what? sun gon' shine

RON: you don't understand

MUTHA WIT: clouds still hover

RON: gramps. everything leads up to this everything i've ever done ever means nothing if i can't put this together the right way

17

MUTHA WIT: this thesis thang?

RON: yes. "this thesis thang"! for some reason i got it in my crazy head that Nat Turner was IT. i mean who the hell needs another paper on slavery . . . no offense.

MUTHA WIT: prophet nat.

RON *(Lit. quick.)*: yeah, iii don't know where it came from but i can't git it outta my head and i have nothing new to say about him or slavery there's nothing new about the fact that he lost his mind and started slashin' folks and okay we survived OKAY ALREADY i mean so what throughout history millions of people have survived horrible events and american slavery is MINUTE when you think about it in terms of what happened during the Crusades and even the uh i don't know i mean turner's revolt was NUTHIN compared to how those brothas and sistas were kickin' up in Haiti okay nat turner/slavery BIG DEAL move on but it won't let me Go!!

fuck!

MUTHA WIT *(Quiet)*: ronnie—

RON: i'm sorry gramps! . . . sorry i . . . listen i need to get back to new york get back to my books so—

MUTHA WIT *(Quiet)*: ronnie—

RON: yes? gramps?

MUTHA WIT *(Quiet)*: . . . ya brain busy 'bout nat.

RON *(Exhausted)*: yes. gramps. very busy.

MUTHA WIT: i sat
and I waited

RON: gramps.

MUTHA WIT: i waited 75 years sayin' nuthin ta nobody barely movin' even I waited 75 years fo' you to be born then I waited 25 mo' years fo' this moment fo' you ta understand the favor I need ta ask ya.

RON: you waited 100 years to ask me what kind of favor Gramps?

MUTHA WIT: I—

RON: note I do have a plane to catch so we may have to cut our little chitchat short and save it for your next birthday.

MUTHA WIT: take me home ronnie.
>Drive me. Carry me. Push me. Take. Me. Home. Home . . .

RON: Gramps you are at home yo' bed is right in the other room I'm about ta put you in it and guess what? when you wake up you will still be at home believe me let's go.

(HE begins to push T.J.)

MUTHA WIT: Me.
>We.
>Slaves.

RON: yeah. i know gramps that's real nice dear. bedtime now.

MUTHA WIT: Prophet Nat.
>Mama.

RON *(Still pushing)*: that's just lovely.

MUTHA WIT: HOME. INSURRECTION. PROPHET NAT.

(RON stops.)

RON *(Quiet)*: . . . oh my god . . . tonight? the vision? in the back? the reporter? and Nat Turner? tonight? they were in—

MUTHA WIT: JERUSALEM.

RON: Jer—
>Jerusalem.
>Jerusalem, Southampton, Virginia.

MUTHA WIT: INSURRECTION.

RON: YES!
>The Insurrection in Southampton.
>Gramps

MUTHA WIT: I. was. there.

(long pause.)

RON: my. thesis.

(silence.)

(Smiling): gramps?—

MUTHA WIT: you got a plane ta catch don't ya?

RON: Tell me!

MUTHA WIT: thought we was cuttin' this li'l chitchat short.

RON: gramps. i'm going to git my tape recorder from my suit-
case it's just out in—DON'T MOVE.

*(Ron exits.
He enters.)*

damn no one can hear but me in my head
no problem no problem Ron calm down I'll remember
I'll remember every single detail every word I'll
remember
or I'll kill myself

(He embraces T.J.)

(Quick): holding history. i'm holding history in my arms
Gramps
SPEAK.

On The Road

Hertz Rent A Car.

RON *(Too sweet)*: Where are we going Gramps? hmm?

MUTHA WIT: Home.

RON: We are in the middle of nowhere we are on a road to
nowhere gramps

MUTHA WIT: turn here

RON: I am driving to nowhere in a

MUTHA WIT: left here

RON: Hertz Rent A Car that is due back in two hours
MUTHA WIT: along there
RON: a plane that has left a connection that I've missed
MUTHA WIT: keep straight
RON: where are we going?!

(beat)

MUTHA WIT & RON: Home.

> *(Suddenly, WHITE SPIRITS and BLACK SPIRITS appear,*
> *BATTLING, around the car.*
> *Ron swerves so as to not hit any of them.)*

RON: Gramps do you see what I—
MUTHA WIT: Yes.
RON *(Bright)*: okay good just checkin'.

> *(Ron swerves once more.*
> *POLICE sirens.*
> *RON pulls over.*
> *SPIRITS disappear.*
> *MUTHA WIT and RON Argue AS*
> *COP appears.)*

COP: Let me see your license.
RON: i thought I was gonna hit those ghosts fighting
      that's all I was trying to do
      to not hit any of them.
COP: You saw Ghosts.
RON: Yes.
COP: Fighting.
RON: Yes.
COP: And you were trying not to hit them.
RON: Yes.
COP: How many drinks have you had?
RON: I can't remember exactly I'm just taking my Gramps
      here home he's had a big day.

COP: And where is his home.

RON: I don't know I mean I I

COP: Step outta the car please.

RON: Officer really I can explain kinda I'm a Ph.D. candidate at Columbia University

COP: Step outta the car please.

RON: my major is Slave History and my Gramps here was a slave so

COP: I won't tell you again to step—

RON: he's 189 years old he can only move his left eye and his middle—

COP: Outta the car!

RON: okay.

MUTHA WIT: Tell 'im we gats thangs ta do.

RON: What?

MUTHA WIT: Tell 'im we don't have no time fo' this mess.

RON: Are you outta your mind—

MUTHA WIT: Tell 'im.

(The COP grabs RON.)

COP: I tried to be nice but—

MUTHA WIT: GET YO' HANDS OFFA MY GREAT. GREAT. GRANDSON.

(pause
The COP looks at RON for a moment.
The COP backs up.
He disappears.)

RON: he's going back to his car to call in the troops we're in the middle of nowhere they're gonna lynch us they're he's leaving he's he's waving good-bye

MUTHA WIT: Wave back.

(RON does.)

Smile.

(RON does.)

Now start this car up and let's go.

RON: I don't know where we are—

MUTHA WIT: I do—

RON: I don't know where or why I'm going to wherever I'm going I hate these dark country roads because they inevitably have white country people living near them all you can say is HOME HOME HOME I've explained to you my thesis and my interest in Nat Turner's Insurrection you know I need to find out about

MUTHA WIT: You a faggot ain't ya?

(beat)

When was you plannin' on tellin' me?

RON: Excuse me?

MUTHA WIT: When was you plannin' on tellin' me? You tol' yo' cousins didn't ya?

RON: Yes.

MUTHA WIT: Yo' Aint Gertha know don't she?

RON: Yes.

MUTHA WIT: Everybody at that party today they know don't they?

RON: Yeah.

MUTHA WIT: Even that reporter know don't he?

RON: Probably.

MUTHA WIT: So when was you plannin' on tellin' me I'm not altogether blind . . . yet.

RON: I wasn't plannin' on telling you

MUTHA WIT: Why not?

RON: I don't quite know if I feel completely comfortable talking to—

MUTHA WIT: you not comfortable boy you know when I knew you was a faggot 22 hours I knew when you was just 22 hours old you popped outta Lillie and the next thang I knew she had you stuffed in my face cryin' 'bout how

cute you was I knew then 22 hours was all it took not
even a full day old.

*(Beat.
mo' Beat.)*

RON: . . . and back to Nat Turner—
MUTHA WIT: Let's talk 'bout Faggots first—

(RON brakes car.)

RON: Look.
Gramps.
MUTHA WIT: What?
RON: I know you ain't been ALL here these past 100 years I
know you've been busy waiting on me and everything
BUT
Only Faggots are allowed to call each other Faggots.
No. body. else.
MUTHA WIT: I heard lotsa folks that weren't no faggots call-
in' each otha faggots
RON: Well they're not allowed to now.
MUTHA WIT: why not?
RON: just call me Ronnie lak you've always called me ronnie,
okay?

(Ron begins to Drive again.)

MUTHA WIT: Ronnie?
RON: Yes Gramps.
MUTHA WIT: You lak ta have men lak that cop fella sit in yo'
lap sometimes?
RON *(Threat)*: hush.
MUTHA WIT: I thought you wanted ta know everythang?
RON: I do but—
MUTHA WIT: So you want me ta tell you everythang but you
don't wanna tell me nuthin you ain't comfortable.

RON: Gramps it's not that—

MUTHA WIT: Then what is it then you go round tellin' everybody but me I thought we was buddies

RON: We are buddies, gramps

MUTHA WIT: Then why you left me out?

RON: I didn't leave you out—

MUTHA WIT: You left me outta it Ronnie! just lak all them
other fools leave me outta it 'til it's time fo' 'em to sho'
back up at my party.

RON: . . . those people care about you a whole lot.

MUTHA WIT: Don't change the subject.

RON: I'm not changing the subject.

MUTHA WIT: Is it fun?

RON: . . . is it fun?

MUTHA WIT: Yeah. Is bein' a faggot fun?

RON: I'm sure I don't know what you mean.

MUTHA WIT: How many years you been at that book learnin'
and you don't even know what fun mean? it mean lak
havin' a nice time lak if you was ta—

RON: I know what fun means gramps.

MUTHA WIT: Then why don't you just answer my question?

RON *(He thinks)*: it is . . . fun . . . at times . . .

MUTHA WIT: Then what?

RON: Huh?

MUTHA WIT: Then what about the otha times when it ain't
fun?

RON: It's not fun being alone, gramps

MUTHA WIT: You ain't alone I'm wit ya.

RON: I mean
at the times
when you're not with me gramps
I'm alone
most of the time

(MUTHA WIT TOUCHES RON.)

MUTHA WIT: i'm still wit ya even when you ain't 'round me.

(RON smiles.)

RON: . . . thanks gramps

(NAT TURNER and a FEW INSURRECTIONISTS cross through the woods in front of the Hertz Rent A Car. They carry AXES, HATCHETS, etc . . . pause)

I'm not seeing this—
MUTHA WIT: PROPHET—
RON: You're not seeing this—
MUTHA WIT: NAT!
follow them!
ova there!!
RON *(Reading above)*: SOUTHAMPTON
COUNTY.

(They pull into a rundown MOTEL.)

Yes.
Rest.
Sleep.
MUTHA WIT: Home.

--- Motel

RON: Excuse me?
Excuse me?
Excuse me?

(CLERK HUSBAND appears.)

CLERK HUSBAND: May I help—

> *(deep)* What you want 'round these parts heah nigga?

RON: Excuse me?

> I must have heard you wrong
> let's try that again

> *(beat.*
> *CLERK HUSBAND exits.)*

> excuse me?
> excuse me?

> *(CLERK HUSBAND reenters.)*

CLERK HUSBAND: . . . may I help you sir?

RON: oh

> yes
> you may I need a room for me and my gramps.

> *(CLERK HUSBAND gets Register.*
> *NAT TURNER appears behind CLERK HUSBAND with*
> *Hatchet.*
> *RON screams.)*

CLERK HUSBAND: What?!

> What is it what?!

> *(RON points behind CLERK HUSBAND.*
> *NAT motions for RON to keep quiet.*
> *CLERK HUSBAND looks behind him AS*
> *CLERK WIFE appears.)*

> That's just my wife the Missus I know she don't look too
> well at this time of mornin' but believe you me she's
> human.

RON: oh

> I'm sorry ma'am I've been drivin' for hours

CLERK WIFE: Name.

(NAT TURNER motions for other INSURRECTIONISTS who all appear and surround the CLERKs.)

Name
Son
you gat a name don't ya?
RON: Ron. Ronald. Porter.
CLERK WIFE: Is that yo' grandpa there?
RON: Yes Great-Great-Grandfather.
CLERK WIFE: Oh how nice.
CLERK HUSBAND: Credit Card or Cash.

(CLERK SON appears with HAMMET holding a Weapon over Him.)

CLERK SON: i heard somebody scream pa y'all okay?
CLERK HUSBAND: That was just Mr. Porter heah Jr. he caught a sight of ya ma.

(The INSURRECTIONISTS move in Closer.)

RON: You people don't sense anything do ya?
CLERK HUSBAND: Anythang lak what?
RON: you people don't see nuthin comin' do ya?
CLERK WIFE: Nuthin but you Mr. Porter now it's early for all of us do you want to pay cash or charge it?
RON: Cash
how much?
CLERK HUSBAND: For a double
CLERK SON: 35 bucks and we gat Cable with HBO n' ESPN as well as bein' fully air-conditioned.
RON: Really.
CLERK SON: Really.
CLERK WIFE: Howard Jr. heah is learnin' the business you know ta take ova from his ma and pa.

CLERK SON: yep i is.

CLERK WIFE: I "am" son and it's "Dollars" not "Bucks" you can go'n back to sleep now everythang's okay heah.

CLERK SON: Yes'um.

(CLERK SON is dragged off by HAMMET.)

CLERK HUSBAND: Room 3F on the left-hand side when you turn the corner in the back it's right in the middle.

CLERK WIFE: Looks lak yo' grandpa don' already hit the hay.

RON: Yeah I should git him inside thank you.

CLERK WIFE & CLERK HUSBAND: You welcome.

(RON turns to leave.
The INSURRECTIONISTS Close In Tighter.)

(Deep low) JIGABOO.

(RON spins around as INSURRECTIONISTS Attack the
CLERK FAMILY, Dragging them kicking and screaming into
the Darkness.
HAMMET reenters.
RON stares at him.
HAMMET motions for RON to come to him.
RON doesn't move.
HAMMET motions again.
RON looks around)

RON: . . . me?

(HAMMET nods and motions once more.)

You wouldn't perhaps be willing to answer a silly question like "who are you? what just happen? have i gon' crazy?" would you?

(HAMMET motions.

29

RON begins to move towards him, involuntarily.)

... uh could you explain how it is I'm moving uh in your direction without wanting to uh move ... in ... your ...

(HE has reached HAMMET.)

... hi ...
I'm—

(HAMMET motions at RON's mouth which opens fully, again involuntarily.
RON is helpless.
Slowly, Silently, Gently HAMMET blows Sweet Air into RON's open mouth.
He motions to RON's mouth again and it closes.
HAMMET smiles.
He disappears.
RON tries to Speak
but no words form.)

II

RON is putting T.J. to Bed.

RON: gramps. enough. okay. i don't know what's goin' on and fo' the sake of my sanity i'm not particularly interested in finding out that information this evening i'm very tired okay? so we gon' chalk all this up to 1 drink 2 many fo' me and 1 life 2 long fo' you i'm puttin' you to bed and when we wake up we're going back home it was *cute* fo' a moment but no more ghosts no more cops no more faggot questions no more craziness good night ... don't let the bed ... bugs ... bite

(beat.)

gramps?
you hear me gramps?

(No Answer.)

Grandpa
Granddaddy
Granddaddy
you still there oh gawd granddaddy you hear me please
don't please . . .

(RON checks T.J.'s Eye.)

Gramps?!

(HE checks his toe.)

Granddaddy!

(He Listens to his Heart.
He hears Singing coming from it.
It is MUTHA WIT's Singing.
SHE sings in the MUTHA TONGUE.)

oh gawd thank you thank you gawd thank you you're
still here gramps i love you you're still here

(MUTHA WIT's Song fills the Space.
RON and T.J. Sleep.
The Song Moves the Bed.
The Song Lifts the Bed.
The Bed Flies upon the Notes.
The Rhythm Surrounds the Bed and
*   it Soars*
*   it Rocks*
*   it Travels*
*   BACK.)*

Plantation

The MO'TEL Farm.
The BED has landed.
It Rests upon the Back of a DEAD SLAVE OWNER, who is MASSA MO'TEL.
The MO'TEL SLAVES, who were in the middle of their Cottonpickin' STARE at the DEAD SLAVE OWNER and the 2, still sleeping, passengers, RON and T.J.
DEAD SILENCE.
Various Slaves are equipped with Shackles, Neck locks, Neck rings, Masks and Bits. A few if not all are chained together. MUTHA WIT is now a crippled slave, named simply MUTHA. also there is a PO' WHITE TRASH indentured servant, named BUCK NAKED.
MO' DEAD SILENCE.
A Slave woman, IZZIE MAE, weary, moves, barely, closer to DEAD MASSA MO'TEL. She bends, almost, to the ground. She blows lightly at DEAD MASSA MO'TEL.

HAMMET: Izzie?

IZZIE MAE: Huh.

HAMMET: Izzie?

Is he dead?

IZZIE MAE: uh-huh.

OMNES: YEEEAAAHHH!!!

(T.J. and RON Awaken.
T.J. is now the same age as his Great. Great. Grandson, and like RON he is a handsome fit young man.
With his own voice, T.J. bellows.)

T.J.: HOME!

(The Slaves begin a FULL-THROTTLE, NO-HOLDS-BARRED, 11:00, BROADWAY, SHOWSTOPPING, BRING

DOWN THE HOUSE, PRODUCTION NUMBER, Chains and all.
SONG: "HE'S DEAD")

SLAVES:
take these chains offa me
unlock these bolts from 'round my feet
that there bed landed on his head
nah cain't nobody tell us massa ain't dead
no mo' ya'suhs from this heah slave
quick niggas com' on let's dig his grave
these cottonpickin' fingers git mighty weary
but they still turn and wave so long dearie

(Chorus)

yeah!!!
ouuuu
he's dead *(5x)*

solid-rock dead
dead as a skunk

from head ta toe my body aches
my bent black back's about to break
my sunburnt neck's gat a permanent crook
he took my child befo' I gat a good look
he sold my mama to a man named John
he raped my sista just fo' fun
he beat my father both black and blue
if he had the chance he'd fuck you too

but!!!
ouuuu
he's dead *(5x)*

(dance break)

33

lainruc

not catatonic or merely sleepin'
if ya take one sniff ya com' back weepin'
his skin is rottin' his lips are cold
this song is endin' nah you been told
that cracker chalky pastey paleface peckerwood red
    neck ofay hick
honkey hoogie blue-eyed devil
IS DEAD
YEAH!!!

(MISTRESS MO'TEL appears.
DEAD SILENCE.
MISTRESS MO'TEL gives the Slaves a knowing glance BUT
doesn't see DEAD MASSA MO'TEL.
SHE SPOTS KATIE LYNN, WHO CARRIES A BABY.)

MISTRESS MO'TEL: Katie Lynn? Katie Lynn?

KATIE LYNN: Yes'um?

MISTRESS MO'TEL: Ain't I don' tol' you 'bout hangin' out 'round these heah common field niggas yousa house niggra and yous need ta start ta 'ppreciate mo' what it mean ta be my house niggra you ain't gon' com' 'round my chile stankin' and sweatin' lak some dog my li'l Wretched Jr. needs a nice cool clean titty ta put in he mouth and I ain't aimmin' fo' 'im ta catch none of these heah dirty-nigga diseases cos yous too stupid ta stay outta the sun.

KATIE LYNN: Yes'um.

MISTRESS MO'TEL: down heah rollin' and runnin' 'round wit these heah common field niggas . . . hmmph . . . you seen Massa Mo'tel?

KATIE LYNN: No'um.

MISTRESS MO'TEL: What 'bout you Hammet?

HAMMET: No'um I ain't seen 'im since early this mornin'.

MISTRESS MO'TEL: Has anybody seen Massa Mo'tel come byheah lately?

OMNES: No'um. Uh-uh. Not me. Not a sight no' hair of 'im. Not one time. NAW.

MISTRESS MO'TEL: Well when y'all do tell 'im I'm lookin' fo' 'im back up at the house.

OMNES: Yes'um. I'll do that. Sho nough. Soon as I sees 'im.

(MISTRESS MO'TEL turns to leave.)

MISTRESS MO'TEL: Izzie Mae what was all that racket I heard out heah a li'l while back.

IZZIE MAE: Nuthin.

MISTRESS MO'TEL: Don't you tell me nuthin niggra don't you come ta open yo' mouth ta a lie ta me gul.

IZZIE MAE: It wasn't nuthin but—

MISTRESS MO'TEL: Nuthin BUT ain't I don' tol' you 'bout everytime I ask you a question you come out with a "Nuthin BUT" if it was a "Nuthin BUT" then it was a SOMETHIN'.

IZZIE MAE: We was just Sangin' Mistress Mo'tel.

(SLAVES SING.)

MISTRESS MO'TEL: Sangin' what y'all gat ta be sangin' 'bout ain't 'nough cotton out heah fo' y'all ta concentrate on?

IZZIE MAE: I mean we was just Hummin' that's all.

(SLAVES HUM.)

MISTRESS MO'TEL: Hummin'?

IZZIE MAE: Moanin' I mean.

(SLAVES MOAN.)

MISTRESS MO'TEL: Y'all keep all that Moanin' down Katie Lynn put li'l Wretched Jr. ta sleep y'all know that boy needs his noon nap and I needs me a li'l peace and quiet fo' a while.

OMNES: Yes'um.

(MISTRESS MO'TEL begins to leave again.)

MISTRESS MO'TEL: BUCK!

BUCK NAKED: Yes'um?

MISTRESS MO'TEL: BUCK NAKED PUT THAT BED BACK
WHERE YOU GAT IT FROM I KNOWS YOU THE ONE
THAT BROUGHT IT OUT HEAH YOU THE LAZIEST
NIGGA I GAT.

BUCK NAKED: Yes'um.

(MISTRESS MO'TEL disappears.
pause)

MUTHA: T.J. I thought you ran off the otha day Massa didn't
even know you was gon' and heah you com' back heah
you a fool and a half to sho' back up heah who dis?

T.J.: . . . mama this heah is . . . Faggot . . . he a friend I met in
the woods we came back cos he heah Prophet Nat gon'
try somethin'.

(NAT appears, in another Reality, NOT seen by anyone except
RON, and T.J.)

MUTHA: He always tryin' somethin' that ain't nuthin new.

KATIE LYNN: Few months ago he was suppose ta do somethin' but he gat sick had all these people waitin' fo'
somethin' to happen talkin' 'bout we made him sick cos
niggas can't git tagetha on nuthin he gat sick July 4th it
was suppose ta be July 4th.

(NAT prays.)

IZZIE MAE: Gittin folks all riled up havin' us gatherin' picks
sortin' axes he only tol' a coupla peoples but word gat
out quick 'bout what he wanted ta do—

(The Sky turns to Night.
The Moon appears.)

BUCK NAKED: —com' tellin' us how that day the moon was turnin' colors

(The Moon changes colors.
NAT watches it.)

IZZIE MAE: say it was a sign fo' him fo' us ta rise up nah he had run away but just lak you fool he came back say he had him some visions

(It THUNDERS.)

MUTHA: Somethin' 'bout BLACK and WHITE Spirits fightin' each otha—

(BLOOD begins to pour from the sky.)

BUCK NAKED: —say he see little people and numbers in front of 'im made of blood I tol 'im ta go see Massa and ask if he could send fo' Docta Simpson 'round the way ta check 'im out ta take a look at 'im.

IZZIE MAE: —he ain't want none of that he say he fine he say he come back heah cos he and us gon' rise up

BUCK NAKED: and kill every white-faced person heah in Southampton.

KATIE LYNN: Y'all rememba that
Crazy Nat?!

IZZIE MAE: his massa musta knocked 'em upside he head 1-2 many times

BUCK NAKED *(Mocking)*: "I SEEN IT I SEEN IT Y'ALL
BLOOD.
SPIRITS.
NUMBERS!!"

(OMNES laugh again except HAMMET and RON, who can't seem to take their eyes off of each other.
AS the OTHERS continue to Laugh and Joke
NAT turns to HAMMET.)

NAT: they don't know. they don't know how it go i spoke ta my maker ya understand.

(HAMMET crosses to NAT.
RON witnesses this.
T.J. witnesses RON.)

HAMMET: i understand prophet. they don't know.

NAT: i been hearin' thangs readin' thangs rumblins from up no'th people up there ready to help once we start

HAMMET: they know 'bout us?

NAT: some of 'em writin' 'bout how slaves lak us all over the place ain't gon' sit still much longer white folks down heah been warned.

(NAT takes out a crinkled corner of an old newspaper.)

this com' from a newspaper last time i ran i caught up wit a man sellin' papers i stole one offa 'im there big as day hammet right there . . . they been warned . . . they been warned by they own peoples

HAMMET *(Smile)*: but it's too late fo' 'em nah.

NAT: paper say they oughta straighten up do right by us o' ain't no tellin' what might happen and what these folks in southampton don't know is i'm "what might happen"

HAMMET: amen.

NAT: you fit?

HAMMET: . . . i'm fit.

NAT: you been studin' 'em letters?

HAMMET: i been studin' 'em

NAT: let me see one 'em A's then.

(HAMMET moves to NAT's Back.
With his Finger he begins Drawing the letter "A.")

HAMMET *(Slowly)*: . . . arrow.
     . . . stick.

NAT: nah do me one 'em B's.
HAMMET *(Concentrates)*: . . . stick.
 . . . rock. rock.
NAT: do that one again and don't speak it this time.

*(HAMMET thinks. then begins drawing AS
he does he still speaks BUT
he makes sure NAT can't hear him.
as HAMMET finishes his 2nd "B"
NAT turns around to him.
HAMMET smiles confidently.)*

okay nah befo' we split i'm gon' teach you a new one.

(NAT begins drawing the letter "C" on HAMMET's Back.)

moon.
this letter "C."

(he points to sky)

think "see" "moon."
"C."
sounds like
KATIE LYNN: Crazy. Nigga.

(SLAVES LAUGH.)

HAMMET: he ain't no crazy nigga nigga! Prophet Nat tol' a
 white man 'bout this stuff he seen say the white man
NAT: Etheldred T. Brantley.
HAMMET: eyes pocked outta his head he
NAT: ceased his wickedness Blood oozed down his skin
HAMMET: say the white man didn't eat he prayed fo' seven
 days straight and
NAT: he was healed.
HAMMET: And then he says he saw the
NAT: SPIRIT

KATIE LYNN: —again
HAMMET: and the
NAT: SERPENT
HAMMET: was loose and he had ta
NAT: FIGHT
HAMMET: Because it's about time fo' the
NAT: FIRST
HAMMET: To Become the
NAT: LAST
HAMMET: And the
NAT: LAST
HAMMET: To Become the
BOTH: FIRST.

(NAT DISAPPEARS.)

IZZIE MAE: What eva 1st last 3rd 5th i don't know but if ya ask me we don't need no half-ass hot-collared nigga-crazy plans 'bout a bunch of axe-carryin' fools creepin' through the streets

KATIE LYNN: we all wants ta be free but we ain't dumb 'nough ta think we gon' be able ta kill all these white folks heah in Southampton and live ta tell 'bout it.

IZZIE MAE: y'all heard what they did ta that funny-looking bad-tempered nigga ova there on the Bowman farm

KATIE LYNN: strung his black ass up in the nearest tree they could find and burnt the skin offa his back

IZZIE MAE *(To HAMMET)*: nah how we know the reverend pastor preacha prophet Nat ain't gon' git out there and start ta seein' none of his li'l blood pictures and freak out on us

KATIE LYNN: i'll tell ya how we know cos befo' he git his chance ta freak out they gon' shoot 'im 'tween the eyes and not worry 'bout findin' 'im no rope

BUCK NAKED: We may have oura picks and hoes and hatches and everythang but I ain't seen no nigga on this farm or any otha outrun no shotgun bullet yet.

HAMMET *(Violent)*: first last last—

IZZIE MAE & KATIE LYNN: nigga please!!

KATIE LYNN: that slogan gat old 6 scenes ago.

T.J.: We just come back ta hear what the man gats ta say that's all ain't no harm in that we just wanna see fo' oura selves.

MUTHA: That's yo' problem you too hardheaded you don't wanna believe shit stinks if ya run off RUN and don't stop till ya cain't run no mo' o' 'til 'em dogs catch up wit ya I always tried ta tell ya wasn't I always sayin' ta "See my foot you'll learn See my foot!"

IZZIE MAE: what's that?!

BUCK NAKED: what?

IZZIE MAE: that smell I knowed I smelled somethin' smelled it ratt after that last musical number.

(ALL the Slaves, except HAMMET, drop to the ground and sniff.
HAMMET crosses to RON.)

HAMMET *(Whisper)*: tonight Prophet Nat's havin' a meetin' Beauford cabin on the O'Hara plantation 10 miles down the way

RON: didn't I see you earlier

HAMMET: we plannin' it tonight

RON: didn't you blow in my mouth

HAMMET: First. Last. Last. First.

RON: Wait a minute. Who. are. you?

T.J.: White Man!

HAMMET: Tonight.

IZZIE MAE: Ova Seea Jones!

KATIE LYNN: How far!

BUCK NAKED: 72.4 feet away!

IZZIE MAE: And comin' Strong!!

(There is a Flurry of Cottonpicking as Slaves try to get enough Cotton for the weight minimum.

A few Slaves fight over Cotton branches and others fight over sacks.)

MUTHA WIT *(To T.J.)*: you and yo' friend grab up one of 'em extra sacks and start ta pickin' T.J. you ain't new heah Ova Seea Jones find you wit a lite load he strip n' skin ya.

(RON hesitates.)

T.J.: PICK BOY.

(RON does.)

Ova Seea Jones is a Breaka.
RON: what's that?
T.J.: you know how they breaks a wild hoss Ova Seea Jones breaks wild niggas nah you keep ya mouth shut and you'll do fine you don' know nuthin 'bout nuthin when someone say somethin' ta ya you gat that you some dumb nigga I picked up on my way up no'th understand?
RON: yes sir.
T.J.: nuthin bout nuthin.
RON: yes sir.

(beat.
Ova Seea Jones appears.
He carries a Whip, a Bucket of Water and a Digital Scale.
The Picking Pace Heightens.
Ova Seea Jones blows a Whistle.)

OVA SEEA JONES: Water Break!

(Ova Seea Jones places Digital Scale on the ground.
The Slaves glare at it.)

It don't make no mess-ups.
You cain't fool it.
Izzie Mae?

IZZIE MAE: Yes suh?

OVA SEEA JONES: You cain't Fool it.

IZZIE MAE: Yes suh?

> (*A few Slaves and RON proceed to place their sacks onto the Scale and are allowed to dip one hand into the bucket of water ONCE and slurp any water they can catch in their palm. IZZIE MAE approaches the Scale. She puts her sack onto it. It's Not Enough. pause*)

OVA SEEA JONES (*Deep*): Take off that top Niggra.

IZZIE MAE: Yes suh.

OVA SEEA JONES: And that bottom.

IZZIE MAE: Yes suh.

> (*She begins stripping off one layer—then another . . .*)

OVA SEEA JONES: And that other top.

> (*IZZIE MAE continues taking off layers of Clothing through the following:*)

Nah
Izzie Mae.

IZZIE MAE: Yes suh?

OVA SEEA JONES: Ev'ryday Ev'ryday I come heah a li'l after noon ta give out water ta you and these otha Niggas so none of ya don't fall out.

IZZIE MAE: Yes suh.

OVA SEEA JONES: And Ev'ryday Ev'ryday you ain't gat yo' minimum done.

IZZIE MAE: Yes suh.

OVA SEEA JONES: We go through the same thang Ev'ryday Ev'ryday don't we Izzie Mae?

IZZIE MAE: Yes suh.

OVA SEEA JONES: how many farms I look after Izzie Mae?

IZZIE MAE: Includin' dis one suh?

OVA SEEA JONES: Includin' dis one Izzie.

IZZIE MAE: Six suh.

OVA SEEA JONES: Six farms!
> Izzie Mae.
> Six farms.
> And all them Niggas on all them Six Farms needs they Sip of Water so none of 'em won't fall out * don't they Izzie?

(* A SLAVE falls OUT. it is the Actress who plays KATIE LYNN.)

IZZIE MAE: Yes suh.

OVA SEEA JONES: And EV'RYDAY EV'RY. GAWD. BLESSED. DAY. I git STUCK on this heah Farm cos I have ta take time outta my what?

IZZIE MAE: Yo' busy schudule suh.

OVA SEEA JONES: My busy schudule on how many farms?

IZZIE MAE: Six Farms includin' dis one suh.

OVA SEEA JONES: Six Farms Izzie Mae I gotta take time outta my busy schudule on Six Farms to do what Izzie Mae?

(No Answer.)

Time Out Ta Do What Izzie Mae?!

(No Answer.)

(Deep): ANSWER ME NIGGRA TAKE TIME OUTTA MY BUSY SCHUDULE ON SIX FARMS TA—

IZZIE MAE: —TA BEAT THE SHIT OUTTA MY BLACK TRIFLIN' STUPID SHIFTLESS NO-COUNT LAZY NIGGRA ASS SUH.

(IZZIE MAE IS NOW STRIPPED NAKED.)

OVA SEEA JONES: That's right.
BUCK NAKED!
BUCK NAKED: Yes suh boss?
OVA SEEA JONES: Tie her ta that Whippin' Post Buck.
BUCK NAKED: Yes suh boss.
OVA SEEA JONES: Tie Her Tight.
BUCK NAKED: Yes suh boss.
OVA SEEA JONES: And her legs too.
BUCK NAKED: Yes suh boss.
OVA SEEA JONES: TIGHT.
BUCK NAKED: Yes suh boss.

(BUCK NAKED ties IZZIE MAE.
TIGHT.
OVA SEEA JONES LIFTS WHIP.)

T.J. *(Low)*: Nuthin 'Bout Nuthin.

(Ova Seea Jones Lashes IZZIE MAE Once.
STRONG.
She Screams.
He RAISES Whip Again.)

Nuthin 'Bout—
RON: MUTHAFUCKA HAVE YOU LOST YO' FUCKIN' MIND!?!

(DEAD SILENCE.)

OVA SEEA JONES: nigga what's yo' name?
RON: . . . Faggot.
OVA SEEA JONES: FAGGOT what did you just say ta me?
RON: I said MUTHAFUCKA—

(OVA SEEA JONES spits in Ron's face.)

OVA SEEA JONES: How you find out I was Fuckin' yo' Mutha boy?

(OVA SEEA JONES Laughs.)

Where you come from Nigga how come I ain't don'
seen you on this heah farm befo'?

T.J.: He from up no'th he one of 'em free Niggas visitin'
down heah wit a friend of Massa Mo'tel's he ain't useta
seein' Niggas beat you know how they do Massa Jones
speak they own minds—

*(OVA SEEA JONES begins to examine RON's Teeth and
Mouth with his Whip.)*

OVA SEEA JONES: Where you git them fancy clothes at nigga
where yo' chains at Faggot?

T.J.: he a free Nigga Massa Jones.

OVA SEEA JONES: T.J. say anotha word and I'm gon' skin you
understand?

(T.J. nods affirmative.)

RON: Whip me
instead of her.

(T.J. Suffers.)

OVA SEEA JONES: You instead of her?
Who you?
Her Savior?
You instead of her.
Take off that Shirt Nigga.

(Ron does.)

And them Pants too.

*(Ron does.
He wears boxing shorts with little designs on them.*

OVA SEEA JONES pokes at RON's Groin.)

Take them funny-looking thangs off.

(Ron does.
He stands Naked.
OVA SEEA JONES examines RON's Face, Teeth, Chest, Groin
and Ass with Whip.)

BUCK NAKED!

BUCK NAKED: Yes suh boss?

OVA SEEA JONES: Buck Naked I want you ta tie Faggot heah
up ta that Post ain't no such thang as a Free Nigga heah
in Southampton.

BUCK NAKED: yes suh boss.

(BUCK NAKED goes to Untie IZZIE MAE.)

OVA SEEA JONES: did i tell you to untie that niggra nigga?

BUCK NAKED: naw suh boss

OVA SEEA JONES: i want you ta tie faggot heah ratt up long
side izzie mae tie 'em tagetha!

(BUCK NAKED pauses.)

pause again nigga and you next.
strip n' skin.

(BUCK NAKED ties RON to IZZIE MAE to the Post.
Slowly.
OVA SEEA JONES hands Whip out to T.J.)

Since you so up ta date on the comin's and goin's on
Free Niggas these days I want ya ta Whip this heah Free
Faggot's Black Ass.

T.J.: Suh?

OVA SEEA JONES: Don't suh me Nigga

pause and you next.
Strip n' Skin.

(T.J. Takes Whip.
He Goes to his Great-Great-Grandson.
He Lifts Whip.)

OMNES: One Hundred Lashes.

(MISTRESS MO'TEL reappears skipping and singing.)

MISTRESS MO'TEL *(Singing)*: ". . . the hills are alive"—Mister
   Jones!? What are you doin'?
OVA SEEA JONES: I'm Breakin' this heah Nigga.
MISTRESS MO'TEL: What if I don't wont that Nigga Broke!?!
OVA SEEA JONES: With all due respect Martha—
MISTRESS MO'TEL: Mistress Mo'tel ta you in front of these
   Niggas Mister Jones.
OVA SEEA JONES: Martha
   with all due respect you don't run this heah farm yo'
   husband do and
MISTRESS MO'TEL: Mr. Jones when I want you ta discipline
   one of my Niggas I'll do lak I always do send them to yo'
   buildin' with a note tellin' you to do just that but I don't
   'llow no Beatin' on my farm up in my face where I can
   see it—
OVA SEEA JONES: Martha!
MISTRESS MO'TEL: MISTRESS MO'TEL.
OVA SEEA JONES: MARTHA
   Yo' husband hired me ta see after this heah Farm nah
   go'n back up in that house there and do lak you always
   do SIT.
MISTRESS MO'TEL: Mr. Jones I want you ta take that Nigga
   down from up offa that Post ratt this very minute and
   Put his clothes back on 'im.
OVA SEEA JONES: This uppity Free Nigga gon' BREAK
   if'n it's the last thang I do.

MISTRESS MO'TEL: I can arrange that Mr. Jones believe me it will not only be the Last thang you do on this heah Farm but it will also be the Last thang you do heah in Southampton.
You're Fired!

OVA SEEA JONES: . . . You cain't fire me Bitch you didn't hire me so you cain't do Shit!!

MISTRESS MO'TEL: Watch.

(she begins to leave in a huff.)

RON: . . . uh! you are Not gonna let him talk to you like that?!

OVA SEEA JONES *(low)*: nigga!

(MISTRESS MO'TEL comes back.)

MISTRESS MO'TEL *(to OVA SEEA JONES)*: you don't know who you talkin' ta I'm gon git my husband down heah ratt quick how dare you come up outta yo' mouth ta me lak that I know all 'bout you you're nuthin but a yella wimp that'll neva 'mount ta nuthin bigga than a nigga whipper.

RON: nigga whipper!

MISTRESS MO'TEL: Nigga whipper!

SLAVES: NIGGA WHIPPER!!

MISTRESS MO'TEL: you must don't know that you Eat because of me and you have the nerve ta disobey me ta call me up outta my Gawddamn Name in front of these heah Niggas! I ain't yo' ev'ryday just slightly above average Southern "dingdong" Belle I may look ta you lak I don't know shit from shinola but without me and othas just lak me you wouldn't be able ta wipe yo' ass clean let alone lay yo' head down in my cabin. . . . IIIIII I mean one of them otha cabins out there on my Farm that's right I said My. Gawddamn. Farm. cos George is as dumb as you when it comes ta what needs to be done when 'round that house up there and this farm down heah IIIIIIIII makes up the moppin' sweepin' dustin' pickin' plowin' choppin' washin' birthin' nappin' eatin' and the Whippin' and the Hirin' and the FIRIN' . . . schedules . . . round heah NOT Massa George Mo'tel he only worry 'bout 2 thangs how much money we make thisa week and how many of these heah Niggra wimmin he can lay wit in thata week So Mister Henry Jacob Jones whose low-life papa and no-life grandpapa worked fo' MY Pappy and MY GrandPappy MISTER!

RON: MISTER!

SLAVES: MISTER!

MISTRESS MO'TEL *(sings)*: MISTER JONES MISTER JONES MISTER JONES MISTER JONES! Yous FIRED.

(She begins to leave.)

(Sings) . . . "doe a dear a female"—

(She Stops.
She Spots the Downed KATIE LYNN.)

katie lynn! katie lynn! get up heifa!

(KATIE LYNN awakens from her faint.
MISTRESS MO'TEL drags her to the Side.)

my husband pass through heah yet?

KATIE LYNN: no ma'am mistress mo'tel.

MISTRESS MO'TEL: when he do be sho n' tell 'im i needs ta speak ta 'im on quick 'bout Ova Seea Jones

KATIE LYNN: yes'um mistress mo'tel

MISTRESS MO'TEL: soons you see 'im . . .

KATIE LYNN: yes'um mistress mo'tel

MISTRESS MO'TEL: i'm weak i'm sooooo weak katie it's too much it's just too much fo' my heart i always try n' treat my help proper nice and gentle but ova seea jones that bed my husband's missin' and the darkies katie them darkies you see how they was lookin' at me they up ta somethin' katie they was gawkin' at me oohhh katie ev'rythangs changin' i'm spinnin' hold me katie i'm spinnin' . . .

(THE WOMEN BEGIN TO SPIN.)

OVA SEEA JONES: . . . nah
STRONG
NIGGA
STRONG.
1!!!

(T.J. Swings Whip
RON Wails.
THE SUN DARKENS
THE EARTH SHAKES)

2!!!

(T.J. Lifts Whip. again.
T.J. Swings Whip
BUT
this time
At OVA SEEA JONES' Throat.
THE SUN SHINES AGAIN.
MISTRESS MO'TEL AND KATIE LYNN STOP SPINNING.
INSTANTLY, The Two Women Change.)

OCTAVIA: Po'lice on the way.
GERTHA: Why they on they way I want them to find Gramps not come heah fo' what?
OCTAVIA: They say he ain't been gon' long enough fo' him ta be missin'.

(T.J. begins to Strangle OVA SEEA JONES with Whip.)

GERTHA: If a 189-year-old man in a wheelchair who cain't and ain't moved in the last 100 years is gon' fo' five seconds HE MISSIN'.

(*Ova Seea Jones TURNS BLUE.*)

OCTAVIA: That's what I tol' 'em but they say they cain't really do nuthin yet but they gon' send a car ova heah soon as they can ta have a look 'round the house.

GERTHA: We already don' don' that.

OCTAVIA: That's what I tol' 'im but they say that's as good as it's gon' git ratt nah.

(*Ova Seea Jones dies.*
T.J. unlocks and unties RON.
T.J. cradles Ron.)

GERTHA: Call and see if Hertz gat they car back from Ronnie this morning somethin' ain't right.

(*PHONE rings.*)

BUCK NAKED: What's that ringin'?

(*The Slaves cover OVA SEEA JONES and the DEAD MASSA MO'TEL in the Bedsheets.*)

GERTHA (*To phone*): Hello.

MUTHA: Buck unlock ya self and take them bodies down to the swamps remember how ta git rid of 'em make sho you cut them pieces no bigga than yo' fist and dunk 'em good and deep and Buck? shut up. live longer. Katie Lynn? Katie Lynn stop daydreamin' gul and you and Hammet git these Sacks tagetha and take 'em on ova ta the gin act lak nuthin happenin' heah ya understand y'all don't know nuthin 'bout nuthin unusual happenin' heah Work Eat Pray Sleep Work nobody don't know nuthin 'bout nuthin else 'cept that and if you feel lak runnin' off you betta think twice 'bout it cos when she find out both Massa Mo'tel and Ova Seea Jones missin' she gon' raise hell and if you missin' too she gon' think in yo' direction and everybody heah know that all a southern white woman lak Mistress Mo'tel gatta do is *THINK* in yo' direction and they'll be after yo' ass with a short rope and a quick hoss nah MOVE.

(BUCK AND IZZIE MAE DRAG OVA SEEA JONES OFF. HAMMET and KATIE LYNN begin loading up the sacks. GERTHA is still on the phone.)

GERTHA: gramps ain't up fo' no follow-up report you was just wit him heah yesterday you did all the interviewin' you gon' do besides you know he cain't talk no-how BYE

(SHE hangs up.
MUTHA mixes Dirt with Water from the Bucket.)

Can you believe that nah you ain't don' hung up from down there at that po'lice station but a good hot minute ago heah he com' callin' me up already Octavia this ain't no time ta be cleanin' up we missin' yo'—

(PHONE Rings Again.)

BUCK NAKED *(Offstage)*: What's that Ringin'?!
GERTHA: Unplug that Gawddamn Phone.
Snatch it outta that Wall Socket.

(MUTHA puts mudpacks on RON's Wounds.)

OCTAVIA: but what if it's Ron callin' mama?
GERTHA: then answer it I ain't heah if it's anybody else.
OCTAVIA *(To phone)*: hello. no didn't. no didn't my mama just tell you he was sitting ratt heah yeah i'm lookin' dead in his face Good-bye Mister Reporter Man see ya next year

GERTHA: see there it gon' be lak that all damn day

(without a beat
GERTHA turns to MUTHA WIT, T.J. and RON.)

MISTRESS MO'TEL/GERTHA: where all them otha niggas
   gon' off ta?

(MUTHA is taken aback by MISTRESS MO'TEL's sudden
Appearance.)

MUTHA: . . . uh massa mo'tel com' bye heah and he tol' us we
   could have the rest of the day off mistress mo'tel
OCTAVIA: you know everybody left last night mama they ain't
   gon' stick around ta clean up nuthin!
MISTRESS MO'TEL/GERTHA: he give y'all the day OFF?!!!!
   WHAAAT!!!????
MUTHA: yes'um mistress mo'tel
OCTAVIA: mama today is SUNDAY everybody got the day Off.

(beat.
MISTRESS MO'TEL Clocks HAMMET.)

MISTRESS MO'TEL/GERTHA *(To HAMMET):* . . . then why
   you still heah?
OCTAVIA: i live heah what you talkin' 'bout I paid my rent fo'
   this month don't start with that nah.
HAMMET: cos i's still gats me a few mo' branches ta pick at
   mistress mo'tel and you know . . . i always lak ta git the
   job done.

(HE makes a Sexual Gesture.
MISTRESS MO'TEL blushes.
beat.
SHE sees the BED.)

MISTRESS MO'TEL/GERTHA: didn't i tell 'em ta git that outta
   heah?

OCTAVIA *(Picking up Digital Scale)*: first you didn't want me ta clean up nah ya do!

MUTHA: massa mo'tel he say that BED should stay cos he say any Nigga claim he too sick ta work can have a bed ta lie down in whiles theys pick cotton wit the rest of us even if theys close ta death he say they still should pick whiles the pickin's good.

MISTRESS MO'TEL/GERTHA: oh.

i guess he ratt bout that . . .

MUTHA: yes'um mistress mo'tel

OCTAVIA: who's right?

GERTHA: What?

OCTAVIA: You said somebody was right 'bout somethin' mama—

MAMA?!

GERTHA: What?!

OCTAVIA: What you wearin'?

GERTHA: What you mean what I'm wearin' I ain't gat time fo' no stupid-ass questions Octavia—

OCTAVIA?!

OCTAVIA: Ma'am?

GERTHA: What you wearin' girl?

(Gertha and Octavia look at each other and then at themselves. pause)

Octavia honey we don' both lost our minds together
Was *Gone with the Wind* on any time last night?

OCTAVIA: No'm not that I know of—

GERTHA: How 'bout *Roots?*

OCTAVIA: No'm—

GERTHA: *Showboat?*

OCTAVIA: Nah-uh I did hear 'em say somethin' bout *The Wizard of Oz* comin' on but I'm not sho—

GERTHA: Are you sho we awake?

OCTAVIA: I don't know last thang I remember was dreamin' 'bout pickin' cotton.

GERTHA: Cotton?

OCTAVIA: That's what I fell ta sleep dreamin' 'bout
this woman that I didn't even know had my body and
was going around pickin' cotton in my dream.

GERTHA: If you was dreamin' bout pickin' cotton then that's
yo' first clue that you needed ta try wakin' yo'self the
fuck up nah let's go check back upstairs one mo' time
cos we might be the ones who gon'.

(They disappear.
MUTHA approaches the WHIPPIN' POST.)

MUTHA: hammet take this trap ta the woods n' burn it

HAMMET: y'all don't need any help wit him

MUTHA: naw go'n do lak i say

(HAMMET moves further off with the POST and
Watches.)

T.J. . . . . T.J. . . . . stop all that fussin' ova that boy you act
lak you ain't never seen no nigga beat befo' you know
Ova Seea Jones lak ta see us whip oura own.

T.J.: I shouldn't brought him heah

MUTHA: I thought he the one wanted ta find out 'bout what
Turner up ta?

T.J.: He was just suppose to watch

MUTHA: Watch what?

T.J.: Watch us.
How we do thangs.

MUTHA: He really ain't no slave?

T.J.: No ma'am
He my buddy.

MUTHA: I don' covered that whip wound he'll be okay.
you plannin' on runnin' again ain't ya?

T.J. *(Looking at her foot)*: you the one taught me how.

MUTHA: when ya leavin'?

T.J.: after the TURNER meeting you know where they
holdin' it?

RON (*Interrupting*): on the o'hara farm.

MUTHA: yeah ova at that "shoutin' beauford" cabin how you know?

RON: . . . um, that guy told me.

(*HE points to the Hiding HAMMET.*)

MUTHA: Hammet you still hangin' round heah git that thang on outta heah boy!!!!

(*HAMMET exits. still looking at RON.
MUTHA turns to RON.*)

MUTHA: you know you favor . . .

T.J.: he don't favor nobody.

MUTHA: nah shut up he favor your Uncle Moses 'bout the head.

T.J.: no he don't

MUTHA: yeah, looks just like him 'bout the head, come here.

T.J.: Mama . . .

MUTHA: see how his head sit back n' UP lak that. if he was comin' at me backwards i'd think it was yo' Uncle Moses, dead on, look.

T.J.: Mama we need ta be goin'

MUTHA: well you ain't hungry o' nuthin?

T.J.: not much ratt nah but maybe we'll stop by after the meetin' on our way headin' no'th.

MUTHA: it would be nice ta say a good-bye ta somebody befo' you go runnin' off again.

T.J.: . . . yes'um.

MUTHA: i'll fix somethin' hot fo' when ya com' through.

(*SHE disappears into WIT.
RON and T.J. remain.
Quiet.
they look at one another.*)

T.J.: that man Ova Seea Jones would've made me kill you boy you cain't act the same heah as you useta Ronnie these are different times different people heah Izzie Mae takes a whippin' everyday boy she gats tough skin she built lak a hoss Ronnie—

RON *(Angry)*: Thats because she's treated like one.

T.J.: i tol' ya not ta say nuthin didn't i? I tol' ya you didn't know "nuthin 'bout nuthin" and what you go and do?

RON: I tried to help her!

T.J.: no you tried ta git kilt!

RON: i thought it was the right thing to do.

T.J.: ain't no right in Southampton boy these niggas heah are slaves you gat that? and whateva these white folks wanna do howeva they wanna do it wit whoeva they wanna do it that make it right.

RON: that's. wrong!

T.J.: what the hell did you think you was gonna see som' picture-book technicolor dream fantasy you on a plantation boy plantations gats slaves white folks treat slaves lak shit and the ones claim they treat they slaves *good* treat they slaves lak *good shit* so nah you brace up and learn ta shut up o' I'm gon' take yo' ass back home ratt nah you gat it? . . . do you understand me Ronnie?

RON: . . . . yes sir.

(beat.)

T.J.: Ronnie you gotta learn yo' place there are times when you say what you gotta say and there are times when you keep all that stuff ta ya'self none of these crackers know what Izzie Mae gat inside her none of 'em don't know what that woman liable ta com' back wit that's dangerous ya see that's what's really scary you don't treat nobody lak an animal beat 'im starve 'im rape 'im take they young from 'im and 'xpect 'im ta lick yo' paw once you com' round ta pettin' 'im lak I said Izzie Mae built lak one of 'em hosses and a hoss'll throw yo' ass offa they back once they load git too heavy so you ain't gotta worry none 'bout Izzie Mae that woman might not be able ta pick her minimum but believe you me she sho 'nough know how much a load she can carry

(Silence.)

nah let's be gittin' on ta that meetin'.

RON: your mother she's— . . . she's . . . she's my great-great

T.J.: great—

RON: grandmother? i gatta talk to her.

T.J.: you cain't talk ta her 'bout nuthin she don't know you from "who don' it?"

RON: but—

T.J.: —that farm is 10 miles away

(IN ANOTHER REALITY, DETECTIVE, OCTAVIA and GERTHA enter.)

DETECTIVE: okay now does he have a last name?

GERTHA: . . . J.

T.J.: you ever walk 10 miles through the woods and swamps?

DETECTIVE: and his first name again was?

OCTAVIA: . . . T.

T.J.: let's go boy by the time I git you there it'll be nightfall.

(They Start Walking.)

DETECTIVE *(Writing)*: . . . T.J. . . . okay—

GERTHA: Excuse me.

DETECTIVE: Yes ma'am?

GERTHA: He ain't in this room.

He ain't in this house.

He ain't on this block.

DETECTIVE: I understand that ma'am.

GERTHA: Then why are you still heah?

DETECTIVE: I just have a few mo' questions that still need to be clarified ma'am.

OCTAVIA: Mister he could've been sold by nah.

GERTHA: Octavia shut up.

DETECTIVE: Anything she can tell me could be helpful in a case lak this go on.

OCTAVIA: . . . He useta be a slave.

DETECTIVE: A slave.

OCTAVIA: Yeah so he's kinda famous

DETECTIVE: i ain't never heard of 'im.

OCTAVIA: . . . he's important to history and stuff somebody might've sold 'im ta somebody else by nah.

DETECTIVE: and exactly what kinda slave was he?

GERTHA: What kind you think?

DETECTIVE: Was this some kinda game that y'all played Ms. Porter?

GERTHA: The man cain't move so how in the hell is he gon' play a game?

DETECTIVE: Well apparently he moved from heah didn't he?

(No Answer.)

Ms. Porter did you ever . . .
beat Mr. T.J.?

(No Answer.)

. . . I mean
in other words what I'm gittin at is did you ever hit Mr. T.J. in order ta achieve some type of sexual gratification?

GERTHA: . . . Are you tryin' ta fuck wit me or just tryin' ta be funny or somethin'?

DETECTIVE: Excuse me ma'am okay excuse me but you people are the ones that called me out heah to investigate some man y'all claim only gat two letters ta his whole name y'all say y'all ain't seen move since y'all been knowin' 'im and he useta be a slave nah you two look lak nice healthy women but there's a lot of crazy folks out heah these days so I gotta ask certain thangs ta know what I'm really dealin' wit heah.

OCTAVIA: Our gramps wasn't no kinda Sex Slave mister he a regular normal everyday Slave

DETECTIVE: Well some of this stuff just ain't addin' up!

GERTHA: Then maybe you cain't add!

DETECTIVE *(To OCTAVIA)*: Fo' instance you been twitchin' every since I gat heah nah ta somebody in my line of bizness them signs that you might be hidin' somethin'.

OCTAVIA: I ain't been feelin' well that's all what you think I gat ta hide I ain't gat nuthin ta hide from nobody!

GERTHA: hmmph.

OCTAVIA: Not even from you mama!

DETECTIVE: Neither one of y'all been able ta explain ta me why y'all dressed the way ya are!

OCTAVIA & GERTHA: WE DON'T KNOW!!

GERTHA: And what does that have to do wit' anything yo' job is ta find my missin' gramps!

DETECTIVE: How I know y'all ain't gat the man down in the basement there huh? strapped ta the washin' machine o' somethin'? ready ta beat Mr. T.J. soon as I leave from heah I mean frankly Ms. Octavia you look lak you might be into a little rough stuff wit them chains and thangs you wearin'

GERTHA: git outta my House!

DETECTIVE: i'm gon' haveta report what i seen heah today back at headquarters y'all know that don't ya?

GERTHA: git outta my house!

DETECTIVE: y'all have a nice day we'll do everythang in oura power ta help see yo' T.J. turns up safe.

(HE exits.
RON and T.J. enter Walking through the Woods.)

RON & OCTAVIA: i'm tired.

GERTHA: mmm-hmmm.

T.J.: see you couldn't have hung 'round me cos i'd been
through these heah woods and back by nah these trails
second nature ta me as many times as my peoples run
through heah

OCTAVIA: ooo and i feel sick.

RON: slow down gramps.

GERTHA: sick? it's called mornin' sickness where i come
from—

OCTAVIA: let me say this one last time
i ain't nowhere near pregnant

GERTHA: yeah okay whateva Octavia

T.J.: i'm the 189-year-old you should be able to keep up wit
that.

RON: i gotta pee gramps.

OCTAVIA: I have somethin' inside of me tryin' ta git out
and it ain't no baby!

GERTHA (Through her teeth): I don't wanna git—

OCTAVIA: you just cain't bring yo' mind to dreamin' that I
might do somethin' with myself beside layin' around
havin' babies stayin' in this backwoods town.

GERTHA: It wasn't backwoods when yo' ass was growin' up
was it and didn't have ta worry none 'bout shoes on yo'
feet o' food in yo' mouth. nah i seen that show you was
lookin' at the otha day had 'em fast-tailed gals talkin'
out the sides of they neck 'bout how theys wimmin nah
that they gat thems a baby i'm the only mama in this
house and i intend fo' it ta stay that way miss woman ya
always been too damn FAST ya need ta

RON: SLOW DOWN!

OCTAVIA: i gats plans!!
whether you believe it or not i'm goin' ta college
i'm gon' make somethin' of myself I'm gon' git out of
this town
just lak ronnie.

T.J.: you so eager to meet and greet turner com' on.

GERTHA: Face it Octavia you ain't as smart as Ronnie!

OCTAVIA: What?!

RON: it's gittin' dark gramps.

GERTHA: Ya ain't ever been and ya ain't ever gon' be!
. . . honey, if the truth hurts grit yo' teefes and bear it . . .

T.J.: we can see oura way by the moonlight don't you worry
keep up we almost there.

OCTAVIA *(Oscar-winning):* . . . this ain't slavery times mama.
I ain't some slave gul on some farm that cain't move
'less somebody tell her she can move
cain't no man take me less I want 'im ta
and I don't haveta pick nobody's cotton
I'm free
ya gat that?
my mind is free
you heah that? mama
my. mind
is. free
ain't that what that commercial say?
i can be ALL i can be?
I can do whateva I set my mind ta do.
I'm not limited
by the people 'round me
and AS GAWD IS MY WITNESS
if I have ta CRAWL—

GERTHA: shut up Octavia and turn on my tv
I wanna see what my soaps talkin' 'bout

OCTAVIA: I don't wanna see no soaps.

GERTHA: It ain't about what you wanna see you still in my
House miss free woman so turn it on.

OCTAVIA: I thought you was so worried 'bout Gramps?

GERTHA: HONEY MY SOAP'S COMIN' ON!!
and when MY SOAP'S COMIN' ON
I don't give a Damn what's happenin' 'round me
so turn my tv set on so i can see if jenny don' had
richard's baby on the side of that cliff where that serial
killer todd who don't know he her half-brother left her
last week

OCTAVIA: . . . that's a shame

(*OCTAVIA mumbles to herself as she turns on TV.*)

* T.J.: . . . shhh . . . shhh . . .
    we heah . . . shhh . . . keep quiet.
* GERTHA: . . . shhh . . . shhh
    Octavia I'm tryin' to watch tv
    wait a minute they ain't about to interrupt my soaps fo'
    no
    News
    Flash
REPORTER: . . . missing 189-year negro t.j.
    last seen with ron porter
    at home of gertha n' octavia porter
OCTAVIA: Mama?
    Ain't that oura street?
GERTHA: It sho look lak it don't it?
OCTAVIA: And ain't that oura house . . . that man looks lak
    he comin' up ta ring—

(*DOORBELL RINGS.*)

GERTHA: You gotta be shittin' me.
OCTAVIA (*To tv*): Look at all them reporters.

(*DOORBELL RINGS again.*)

GERTHA: Octavia honey go ta that window and see if that's
    us.

(*OCTAVIA does.*
AFTER a Moment.
MO' DOORBELL RINGS.)

    Octavia gul you on the TV!
OCTAVIA (*Excited*): I know mama I'm lookin' dead at the cam-
    eras.
GERTHA: you see that reporter man out there?

OCTAVIA: uh-huh he out there!

GERTHA: wait 'til I git my hands on that man. com' on octavia
and don't you open yo' mouth i'll do the talkin' you
don't know nuthin 'bout nuthin.

(THEY Exit.
RON and T.J. remain.
Huddled Tight in the Dark Woods.)

T.J.: Okay
we wait heah 'til folks start comin'.

(silence.)

. . . . so?

RON: . . . . . . so?

T.J.: . . . . you excited?

RON: . . . . I'm exhausted.
I've never walked so far so fast in my whole life.

T.J.: you glad I brought you heah?

RON: yeah, I'm glad. i can't believe all of this—

T.J.: kinda funny ain't it?

RON: you. you're . . . . you're real you're talking you're . . .
gorgeous.

T.J.: hush.

RON: you are. i mean there's so much i want to
so much i wanna ask about i wanna

T.J.: it ain't lak what you read in 'em books is it?

RON: no sir.

(beat.)

T.J.: well we ain't gat all day boy let me have it what ya want
to know make it simple nah i'm still old tho' i may look
brand-new.

(beat.)

com' on boy
SPEAK.

RON: i'm thinking

T.J.: you had 25 years of thinkin' ask me somethin' 'fo these
folk start ta showin' . . . what ya gat on ya mind—

(beat.
RON takes out a NotePad from his BOOKbag.)

RON: oh. yes. i wrote a few questions out uh—

(HE searches the questions he's Written.)

T.J. *(Quiet)*: yeah?

RON: gramps um . . .
do you believe in god?

(silence.)

with everything that happened with the beatings and
burning . . . and the dying . . . and . . . did you come
out of all of it . . . this . . . still believing in god? . . . really
believing?

(beat.
the 189-year-old ex-Slave takes his 25-year-old free grandson in
his ARMS.
the free MAN is extremely uncomfortable.)

(Moving) . . . gramps—

T.J.: shhhhhhshhhhhh . . .

(the ex-Slave Rocks his Grandson.)

shhhhhhhhh
rest.
. . .
you move too much ronnie
you always on the go

settle
rest
shhhhhhh . . .

(RON
eventually
settles.)

wit all the thangs i been through seen all the thangs i don' don' n' i neva held you in my arms befo' you know? now i can now i'm able

(they view the WORLD above.)

RON *(Slow)*: i sometimes wondered what it'd be like . . .
to know you before you stopped
moving
go for walks with you
even if it was just down to the corner candy store and
    back
to sit on your lap and be told how things were
fish drive cook swim
explore . . .
touch

(they HOLD 1 Another.)

T.J.: . . . you know them times in the quiet when ya feel ya'self lift a little? n' ya know there's somethin' there liftin' the weight? at those times when ya know there's somethin' thats holdin' ya steady pushin' ya through carryin' ya ova? ya ever feel that way sometimes ronnie? light on ya feet even in times of trouble?

RON: . . . yes sir. sometimes.

T.J.: then that's somethin' ta believe in.
call it what ya want.

(silence.)

nah i gat a question fo' you did you know by the time I
knew 22 hours?

RON: know what?—

T.J.: 'bout bein'—

RON *(Laughing)*: why are you so interested in that Gramps?

T.J.: why are you so interested in this?

RON: this is my past

T.J.: you my future.

you the one gon' carry my scars.

memba my eye? papa gat his left eye cow-poked out fo'
lookin' at Mistress Mo'tel's younger sister when she was
down heah visitin' a few years back he was pickin' up her
suitcases and by mistake took and looked her in the face
that was all it took poked his eye outta his head and sold
'im down south and my feet? my mama lost all her toes
'cept the middle on the right fo' runnin' away wit me
when I was fo' o' five we carry they scars the longer we
live the mo' it sho' ya understand?

RON: yes sir.

T.J.: shh. i heah 'em they comin' . . .

promise me somethin' ronnie—

RON: i wont say anything this time don't worry gramps i know
"nuthin 'bout—

T.J.: no.

promise me

you be safe

you live in dangerous times

just lak we do heah

so

you be safe

. . . okay?

RON: . . . . i promise

T.J.: you my future.

(T.J. kisses RON.
THEY Wait.)

Nat's Turn

Beauford Cabin on the O'Hara Farm.
NAT Stands above a crowd of Slaves who are Crouched low.
HAMMET Stands next to him with a modern-day Headgear Walkie-
talkie (à la Fruit of Islam and/or The Secret Service)
MUTHA, T.J. and RON are among the Slaves.
HAMMET and RON's eyes rarely move from one another.
IZZIE MAE Stands near the entrance, Praying at the top of her lungs.

IZZIE MAE: LAWD
    I just wanna thank you ONE MO' TIME
    fo' givin' me such a Nice and Kind MASSA
    oh LAWD
    MASSA
    every since my husband
    BEAU B. BEAUFORD
    pass from this heah blessed earth into yo' heavenly arms
    oh LAWD
    MASSA
    BEEN MIGHTY GOOD TA ME
    oh LAWD
    I couldn't ASK you fo' a betta MASSA
    he wakes me at 5:01
    'stead of 5 ta go out in the field
    lak he do the othas
    he only have me beat twice a day
    'stead of fo'
    lak he do the othas
    he take real GOOD care of the 72 kids he have by me
    oh JESUS
    THANK YA
    MASSA BEEN MIGHTY GOOD TA ME
    oh LAWD
    HE BEEN MIGHTY MIGHTY

> MIGHTY MIGHTY
> GOOD TA—

HAMMET: He gon' nah he pass on down the row.
IZZIE MAE: You sho?

(HAMMET yeah.)

> Reverend Pastor Preacher Prophet Nat
> Speak ON.

(The Slaves Stand and applaud.)

NAT: Thank you Izzie I know we can always count on ya ta
Raise Cain when we need 'im now back to the business
at hand
> THE SPIRIT
> SAID UNTO ME
> THE SPIRIT SAID PROPHET NAT
> PROPHET
OMNES: PROPHET
NAT: NAT
OMNES: NAT
NAT & OMNES: SEEK YE THE KINGDOM
> OF HEAVEN
> AND ALL THANGS
> SHALL BE ADDED
> UNTA YA

(the Slaves ad-lib Down-Home-Baptist-Style.)

NAT: NAH EV'RYBODY IN HEAH
KNOW I AIN'T CRAZY

(DEAD SILENCE)

> Y'ALL KNOW
> THAT I AIN'T CRAZY

LAK THE WHITE MAN
* TRY TA TELL ME I AM

(* *SLAVES git back in the groove of thangs.*)

COS YA SEE
WIT MY PLOUGH
IN MY HANDS
I BENT
MY HEAD
I BENT
MY KNEES
AND I CALLED
JESUS
JESUS
GIVE A SIGN
JESUS
ANY OL' LI'L SOM'THIN'
GIVE ME THAT ONE SIGN
AND I'LL MOVE FO' YA
I'LL WALK FO' YA
I'LL TALK FO' YA
I'LL KILL FO' YA
LAWD
GOOD GAWD ALMIGHTY
HE SHOWED ME
BLACK AND WHITE SPIRITS
TUMBLIN'
IN THE SKY
MEN OF DIFFERENT ATTITUDES
FORMS, SHAPES AND SIZES
THUNDER RANG
SLAVES SANG
LISTEN HEAH GANG
OMNES: Huh?
NAT: I SAW IT
WIT MINE OWN 2 EYES

MY SAVIOR'S HANDS
STRETCHED
STRETCHED
CROSS SOUTHAMPTON
OVA INTA CALVARY
ON UP TOWARDS JERUSALEM
IF YOU DON'T BELIEVE ME
CALL 'IM UP
CALL UP HIS NAME
CALL 'IM UP

BUCK NAKED: WHAT'S HIS NUMBER?!
NAT: 1-800-DIAL-GOD
CALL 'IM UP

'MEMBER THAT ONE NITE
WHEN THE MOON
CHANGED COLORS
THE TREES STARTED SHAKIN'
THE WINDS GAT COOL
THERE I WAS
THERE I WAS
OUT IN THAT FIELD
LABORIN'
IN THAT FIELD
IS THERE ANYBODY IN HEAH?
SAID THERE I WAS
LABORIN'
I LOOK UP
LOOOOKED UP
AND ON THE LEAVES
I SAW FIGURES
DRAWN IN BLOOD
BLOOD
THE BLOOD OF CHRIST

SOME OF Y'ALL DON'T BELIEVE
SOME OF Y'ALL THINK I DON' LOST IT

SAYIN' TA YA'SELF
WELL NAH PO' REVEREND
PASTOR PREACHA PROPHET NAT
HE DON' LOST IT
AIN'T THAT A SHAME
AIN'T THAT SAD

BUT I WANNA LET EACH AND EV'RY-ONE OF YA
    KNOW TONITE
YOU AIN'T GATTA BE SORRY
FOR PROPHET NAT
YOU AIN'T GATTA WORRY NONE
FO' OL' NAT TURNER
COS THE HOLY GHOST
SAID UNTA ME
HE SAID "PROPHET NAT!
FIGHT
FIIIGHT
FIGHT 'GAINST THE SERPENT!"

I REJOICED!

(they do)

I JUMPED UP!

(they do)

STOMPED MY FEET!

(they do)

I PUT MY LEFT FOOT IN!
I TOOK MY LEFT FOOT OUT!
I PUT MY LEFT FOOT IN!
AND I SHOOK IT ALL ABOUT!!

73

I DID THE HOKEY-POKEY Y'ALL
AND I TURNED MYSELF AROUND
'COS YA SEE
THAT'S WHAT IT'S ALLLLLLLL ABOUT

I AIN'T STUPID
AND I AIN'T CRAZY
IIII KNOW
THE REVELATIONS OF THE PLANETS
IIII KNOW
THE OPERATIONS OF THE TIDES
IIIIIIIII KNOW
THE CHANGES OF THE SEASON
AND I CAME HEAH TA TELL YA
TONITE CHURCH
THAT THE TIME
HAS COME
IT'S TIME
TIME
YES IT IS
THOSE OF YOU THAT MURMURIN'
'GAINST ME
YOU OUGHTA KNOW THAT IT'S
TIME
TIME
FO' THE FIRST
TO BECOME THE LAST
AND THE LAST
TO BECOME THE
HAMMET: WHITE MAN!

(The Slaves Drop.
IZZIE MAE shouts.)

IZZIE MAE: MIGHTY MIGHTY
MIGHTY MIGHTY
GOOD TA ME

oh LAWD
MASSA
BEEN MY DOCTA
IN DA SICKROOM
HE BEEN MY LAWYA
IN DA COURT—
HAMMET: he gon'.
IZZIE MAE: that was a close one.

(The Slaves Recover.)

NAT: we don't have ta hide no mo' my Brothas and Sistas! Not after tonite.
HAMMET: what's yo' plan Prophet?

(beat.)

NAT: we gon' take oura tools them picks n' axes n' hatchets n' MARCH ouraselves ratt on up ta JERUSALEM n' ev'ry white face we see we KILL 'em DEAD.

(SILENCE.)

IZZIE MAE: what time you reckon we gon' be through wit the killin' cos my chill'un lak theys dinner 'round 6 we gon' be back befo' that Reverend Pastor Preacha Prophet?
NAT: We Ain't Comin' Back heah!
We Marchin' fo' oura Freedom!
IZZIE MAE: fo' how long tho'?
NAT: fo' Fo'Ever!!
IZZIE MAE: I gat Chill'un ta Feed!
KATIE LYNN: ain't that the same plan you had a month ago fo' July 4th?
NAT: yes i know it is
KATIE LYNN: then you know what happened.
nuthin.
NAT: i gat sick okay? there was nuthin i could do about that.

KATIE LYNN: why couldn't you just call up yo' GAWD and ask 'im ta fix ya up ratt betta since you and 'im so close and friendly speak all the time lak buddies.

NAT: that ain't nuthin ta make no joke at nigga!

IZZIE MAE: how you know you ain't gon' git sick again?

NAT: I KNOW.

IZZIE MAE: HOW?

KATIE LYNN: and why there so few WIMMINS up in heah?

IZZIE MAE: cos they ain't crazy that's why

BUCK NAKED: let the mens handle this we don't need no wimmins and kids slowin' us down.

IZZIE MAE: what you mean slowin' you down I crawl faster than you run what we suppose ta do sit back twiddle oura thumbs and wait hell naw that won't be me *(to KATIE LYNN)* you heah what this po' white trash try n' tell us—

BUCK NAKED *(strong)*: just cos i'm different don't make me no different i'm still a slave just lak yo' black—

IZZIE MAE: my black what!?!

BUCK NAKED *(quick)*: uh . . .

IZZIE MAE: go'n say it! my Black. What. BUCK!?!

BUCK NAKED: . . . uh . . .

(he turns to MEN for support. they got his Back.)

(strong) . . . i don' 'bout heard 'nough outta you Woman!

(dead silence. he checks the men again. they still got his back.)

(negro) i'm not gon have you givin' me word fo' word. i bends just as low picks just as much hauls just as many works just as hard as any otha nigga in heah n' i be damned if'n you gon walk all through me just cos i'm day n' you nite!

(mo' silence.)

IZZIE MAE: ohhh so you wanna talk da talk and walk da walk?! i see nah dat after i don' shouted fo' da lawd you want me to git ugly up in heah *(to KATIE LYNN)* he want me ta git ugly up in heah!

KATIE LYNN: go'n git ugly gul!

IZZIE MAE: MASSA NAKED! what you gon do when one of these otha fools git ta lakin how they feels plowin' through white folks guts n' stuff folks runnin' eva'which-away up n' down stairs in n' outta doors folks screamin' KILL 'IM DEAD!! and they glimpse. YOU. out da corner of they eye n' they turn they 'tention ta yo' White. Ass?!

(beat. BUCK. terrified. considers. this. he turns to MEN for an answer.
NAT goes to BUCK NAKED and IZZIE.)

NAT *(quiet)*: Brotha and Sista Please!

KATIE LYNN *(low)*: nat turner have you lost yo' natural mind?

NAT: I Saw BLOOD!

KATIE LYNN: So!

NAT: I Had VISIONS!

KATIE LYNN: FUCK. VISIONS! we talkin' 'bout the lives and safetys of all these otha niggas up heah in Southampton not just you and yo' hot-blooded crew of Mens.

HAMMET: Calm Down Katie Lynn don't you start—

IZZIE MAE: Naw.

don't Calm her down this CRAZY NIGGA gon' git us all Kilt.

NAT: The HOLY GHOST said—

KATIE LYNN: do you expect ALL these white folks heah ta just sit back and sleep through this whole thang while you go 'round choppin' 'em up?

IZZIE MAE: and i fo' one wanna know what you gat in sto' fo' when they do start ta wakin' UP?!!

NAT: MY GAWD—

IZZIE MAE: Yo' GAWD let these white men Snatch us up from offa that Coast and bring us ova heah.

KATIE LYNN: Yo GAWD let my uncle sell his own Brotha and
Me ta that white man fo' a GUN.

IZZIE MAE: Yo' GAWD let MASSA whip me Raw each and
every chance he com' bye.

KATIE LYNN: Yo' GAWD let 'im take my babies out from up
under me and then let that SAME white man git up Ova
me again ta make some mo' babies.

IZZIE MAE: and yo' GAWD let Yo' Black Ass git Sick on July
4th last.

(SILENCE.
MO' SILENCE DAMMIT.)

KATIE LYNN *(Quiet)*: . . . we need ta think 'bout it somemo'
reverend pastor preacha prophet nat we need ta make
us up a Map and git us some mo' wimmins up in heah
see what they think . . . least . . . that's what me and izzie
mae think . . .

(silence.)

NAT *(Calm)*: . . . izzie mae . . . katie lynn . . . what y'all gon' do
wit a MAP y'all can't even read.

RON: I CAN READ AND I GOT A MAP
I can TEACH you all to Read it!

(THE SLAVES SCREAM IN TERROR.
THEY DROP.
T.J. is in an Absolute State of Shock.
from the ground:)

BUCK NAKED: nigga is you crazy?

T.J.: these white folks skin you 'live boy they heah you talk
'bout teachin' somebody how ta read out loud and open

RON: they'll "skin us 'live" if they find all of us in this shack so
what's the difference we're here to talk so lets talk

KATIE LYNN: somebody shut this fool up befo'—

RON: Look.

60% of the population in this county is Black,
60%

NAT: How you know?

RON: I read it.

(The SLAVES Scream/Retreat in Horror.)

IZZIE MAE: hush yo' mouth 'bout that readin' nigga

RON: I READ IT!

(They Scream/Run Further Away.)

T.J.: ronnie!

RON: look if south africa can get the vote then—

BUCK NAKED: south africa?

nigga we in southampton how you git south africa outta that?

RON: it's the same thing.

KATIE LYNN: they let they slaves vote in south africa?

RON: they're not exactly slaves over there but—

IZZIE MAE: but nuthin

Shut up.

T.J.: nuthin 'bout nuthin!!

RON: i can help gramps!

2 black people can't be in the same room with one another without 1 tellin' the otha to shut up

OMNES: SHUT UP!!

RON: listen Prophet Nat Katie Lynn's right they're gonna kill all of you they're gonna put down your Insurrection send in a couple thousand of their troops kill all of you but I can help we need more time more planning.

BUCK NAKED: ain't you that free nigga i tied up this mornin'?

OMNES: mmm-hmmm.

RON: Prophet Nat they're gonna catch you after 60 days you gon' hide up in trees in dark damp caves under cold hard rocks without food—

NAT: I don' that befo'—

RON: —and then they're gonna catch you and Hang you—

NAT: Brotha—

RON: —and they're gonna whip your wife 'til she's close to her death before she agrees to give up your papers you gotta believe me I Know

(HE PULLS A BOOK OUT OF HIS BOOKBAG.)

I Read It!

(The Slaves GASP.
maybe 1 faints.
Silence.)

NAT: Brotha what is yo' name?

RON: My name?

My name is Ronald Antonio Porter.

I will be receiving a Ph.D. in Slave History next year from Columbia University in New York City and I'm doing my final Thesis on the American Slave Insurrections on people like you Prophet I know that yours is gonna be the bloodiest but these white people are gonna kill

T.J.: don't. ronnie.

RON *(Fierce)*: hundreds upon hundreds!! who had no idea what you were doing you hold the lives of hundreds of innocent people in your hands you can't do this without more preparation you're only going to git to kill a little more than fifty white people they're gonna destroy hundreds of our people you. need. more. time. more detailed fully thought-out planning I can help you I can do that.

(silence.
the PROPHET goes to the FREEMAN.
he takes the book from Ron. he opens it. there is uneasy movement from the SLAVES who pray no one comes into this cabin.
the PROPHET reads the title page.)

NAT: "the CONFESSIONS OF NAT TURNER"

(Nat pauses.)

RON *(Humble)*: . . . if you take a glance inside you'll notice there's maps included . . . uh . . . there . . . they got maps that show exactly the route you took the houses you went to 1st 2nd and so . . . forth . . .

(beat.)

NAT: who dis thomas gray?
RON: . . . he's a lawyer he's a um the slave owner who takes your confessions . . . after . . . uh . . . after they catch you and lock you up.
NAT: i'm suppose to have confessed ta som' white lawyer who owned som' o' my peoples
RON: well not—
NAT: i'm supposed to have tol' this white lawyer i never even heard of all my thoughts all my ideas all my life stories?
RON: . . . we know all of it can't be absolutely true but

(Nat looks to RON.
NAT turns the page.
beat.)

NAT: "having soon discovered to be great. i must appear so. and therefore studiously avoided mixing in society and wrapped myself in mystery devoting my time to fasting and prayer by this time having arrived to man's estate and hearing the scriptures commented on at meetings i was struck with that particular passage which says seek ye the kingdom of heaven and all things shall be added unto you"

(beat.)

this ain't wrote lak i talk
you believe i said what he say i said

RON: not all . . . um not all of it

NAT: this the serpent's work brotha.

RON: prophet in the future where i live

NAT: the future. i've seen the future brotha. i'm the chosen.
the chosen 1 ta see what othas cain't you know that
christ died for yo' sins

RON: no.

NAT: no?! the YOKE!! christ laid down the yoke he had borne
for the sins of men AND MY MAKER TOLD ME TA
TAKE IT UP! and

RON: no. i don't believe that prophet.

(beat.)

NAT: this book.
this devil-work.
if this book is what you believe in
in the future that you live in without a
CHRIST
then that FUTURE that you Livin'
is a LIE

*(he gives BOOK back to RON.
silence.
T.J. GOES TO HIS GREAT-GREAT-GRANDSON)*

T.J.: let's go ronnie—

RON: no.
prophet.
you're living the lie

(NAT looks from RON to SLAVES to RON again.)

NAT *(Quiet)*: you see these bumps on my head

(he rips open his shirt)

you see these marks on my breast
they didn't com' from no man's whip
they didn't com' from no workin' under no sun
i was born wit 'em
theys a sign

RON: you think God showed you the way? you think—

NAT: he. picked. me.
i have no right to question it.

RON *(To SLAVES)*: in the back of this book there are a list of names

NAT *(To SLAVES)*: befo' i could walk as a chile i can remember tellin' otha children thangs

RON: next to them names is a list of owners

NAT: thangs that happened befo' i was even born

RON: NEXT to that is a list of SENTENCES

NAT: my granny say "he right"

RON: DEATH. sentences.

NAT: "he a PROPHET."

(silence.
the 2 men turn to 1 another.
quiet.)

. . . i could read befo' any of my peoples could count

RON *(Holding book)*: then read them their death sentences
prophet

(silence.)

(Difficult) . . . point to the one . . . point . . . to the one
over there who will . . . be burned alive
strapped to a tree trunk
flung
over a branch
with a noose around . . .

    . . . point. prophet.
read. this. list.
tell them.
whose? private parts will be sliced.
off.
fed to some dog while they watch

(beat.)

    . . . more hatred
more brutality
more . . . blood
. . . that's the future prophet
that's the future
that i know

(RON holds BOOK out to NAT 1 last time.
NAT discards the BOOK)

NAT: that cain't reach me.
i'm too high.
don't mean nuthin ta me them words in there cain't
move me cos ya see i gots me a ROCK that i stand upon
the BOOK of Gawd is my foundation the WORDS of
CHRIST is my ROOT
and i'm heah ta tell YOU
I'M. DONE. HEAH.
i've been called n' that's all the preparations I need i'm
done heah.
now I want all of y'all ta go'n back ta ya farms and wait
fo' my signal only tell those you trust nobody else have
ya weapons ready cos soon Soon I'm gon' be comin'
through and I'm not stoppin' fo' nuthin o' nobody 'til
I git ta Jerusalum.
and those of you who wants theys Freedom
Be Ready!

(Nat and the slaves begin to leave, still Crouching low.
RON watches them.
beat.
the SLAVES are All GONE.)

T.J. *(Furious)*: nah what was all that boy!
RON *(Sickened)*: how come you let them go!
T.J.: how come you cain't keep yo' mouth shut!
RON: he ain't GREAT. Nat Turner ain't no more no greater
no higher than any of them others you know that! and
you just watched!! how could you just stand and watch
it!!
T.J.: i LIVED it!!
RON: they WONT!! . . .
they're gonna lose
and you know it
they gonna be massacred
that's losin' gramps
they gonna lose.

(beat.)

T.J.: slavery.
ends.
ronnie.
RON: i know that—
T.J.: HUSH UP!
you know nuthin
you know letters on paper
you know big words
connected ta little ideas
you know nuthin
i killed a man this afternoon
wit'out a thought
wit'out a hesitation
i killed that son of a bitch because it was either him o'
you

and. YOU. mine.
i didn't need no mo' time i didn't need no mo' thinkin'
    i didn't have no plan
DEATH ain't nuthin new ta me n' it ain't new ta them
    slaves
i LIVED it!!
you. the one Watchin'!
i brought you heah ta learn. ta listen. not change nuthin
we change in oura OWN time.
not. in. othas.
you wake up ev'ry mornin' breathin' the AIR that NAT
TURNER fought fo' you ta breathe and you sleep ev'ry
nite wit no FEAR cuz that crazy. nigga. SHOUTED Out at
the Moon askin' his Gawd fo' a way thru dis trouble and
you think you can show up back heah and BLOCK that!!!
ronnie you are who you are because them people that's
gon' git shot up hung up cut up is what will 'llow you ta
enter them doors of that fancy college ya go ta read them
wordy books and write them thesis papers SEE these niggas heah cain't understand that ALL they know is that
they wanna be FREE and that's what they plannin' ta Do
So they gon' WIN
they might DIE
but they gon' WIN
You. da Proof.

(the SLAVE and the FREE MAN
Clock each other.)

slavery.
ends.
. . .

(beat.)

. . . i'm takin' you BACK you sit still in heah i'm gon'
scout the best route out don't. move.

(T.J. Exits.
silence.
HAMMET is revealed in the darkness.)

HAMMET: i shook.

(RON turns to him.)

when i first saw you
i shook.

(silence.
HAMMET slowly goes to RON.
RON stops Him.)

RON: uh . . .
wait a second . . . uh . . . are you . . . do you . . .
you like boys?

(the SLAVE smiles.)

HAMMET *(Quiet)*: . . . i lak you.

(HAMMET Kisses RON . . . lightly
and now it is RON's turn to
FAINT.)

—————————— Some Enchanted Evening

A MAN SINGS.
Deep in the WOODS
NAT TURNER, carrying some foodstuff and a Hatchet,

APPEARS
AS
GERTHA and OCTAVIA (who has a Baby Doll Strapped to Her)
Appear Sneaking through their BACKYARD
NAT *(sings):*
> i had ta pray so hard
> but i'm on my way

> *(THE WOMEN notice HIM and Stand in Shock!*
> *beat.*
> *NAT stops Singing.)*

> where y'all headed?

> *(beat.*
> *the Women stare at his tattered clothes.)*

> huh? where y'all goin'?

OCTAVIA: To find—
GERTHA: Shoppin'.
NAT: It's too early in the mornin' fo' no sto' ta be openin'.
GERTHA: This one heah is open 24 hours.
NAT: I'm tellin' you that ain't no sto' open this time of mornin' nah y'all ain't seen no white folks runnin' round heah have ya? they ain't found out nuthin have they?
OCTAVIA: yeah they know all about it that's why there's a whole street full of them out in front.
NAT: There is?!
OCTAVIA: yeah! that's why we creepin' through heah so they won't see
NAT: why didn't i see no white folks when I came up heah when they git heah?
OCTAVIA: 'Bout fo' o'clock this afternoon just sittin' out there waitin'.
NAT: What?!
> Waitin'?!
> how they find out?!

GERTHA: why don't you run out front there and ask 'em.

NAT: nigga is you crazy?!

GERTHA: naw nigga is you
you the one in my backyard singin' spirituals!

NAT: i'm the prophet, woman!

GERTHA: and i'm the virgin mary, man, nah when do you
FO'SEE yo'self movin' further than my backyard?!

OCTAVIA: Mama remember he the one holdin' the hatchet
let me handle this
mister would you like a dollar or somethin' fo' a meal?

GERTHA *(Through her teeth)*: Octavia honey you ain't gat no
money on you.

OCTAVIA: Yes I do.

GERTHA: YOU AIN'T GAT NO MONEY
and neither do I!

OCTAVIA: then how was we suppose ta be goin' shoppin'?!

(GERTHA cuts Octavia with a deadly glance.)

NAT: any of 'em gat guns.

OCTAVIA: guns?

(sound of a Helicopter invades the space.)

NAT *(Freaking)*: what's dat!!

OCTAVIA: it's just the helicopters they been comin' and goin'
all day long.

NAT: Helicopters?! what dat is?!

GERTHA: That big machine that flys in the sky with the wings
on that spins makes a lotta noise.

(beat.)

NAT: Y'all git on away from me
run on along
keep ya mouth shut you never saw me I'ma go peek how
many they is I gat some mo' folks comin' shortly don't
ya worry.

(He disappears.)

GERTHA: Nah see there Octavia that's what 200 years of Slavery done did ta oura people and you gon' go tellin' him all our bizness offerin' him money THE NIGGA HAD A HATCHET octavia-gul why you carryin' 'round that baby doll wit'cha?

(OCTAVIA notices the Baby Doll for the 1st time.)

OCTAVIA *(Serious)*: i don't know.
GERTHA: gul you ain't got a bit o' the good sense gawd gave ya
let's git outta heah.

(OCTAVIA doesn't Move.)

OCTAVIA *(Quick)*: you know sometimes you treat me lak i'm dumb
GERTHA: are we gon' go through this again—
OCTAVIA: i may not be super smart lak ronnie but i know certain thangs
'bout life
GERTHA: octavia—
OCTAVIA *(Strong)*: i had a baby inside me
. . .
there i said it
i made 'em take it outta me i didn't want no baby slowin' me down gat thangs to do gatta git outta that place we in and i couldn't do that wit no baby so you was *right* but i made 'em *Take. It. Out.*
i'm *smart* mama.
i'm *smart enough* to know THAT.
. . .

(OCTAVIA begins to Exit.
But

GERTHA cathes her Arm . . . and
She HOLDS her Daughter.

this is New *for Both of Them.*
soon.

GERTHA pulls away and starts to EXIT.
she stops.)

GERTHA: *. . . you ain't too far . . . from where i been . . .*

(silence.
OCTAVIA opens her mouth to speak but

GERTHA knowing this is not the time or place for this discussion, EXITS.

OCTAVIA is left Alone.
she ponders her own Mortality.
then
Races off to her Mother.)

─────── Love For Sale/The Last Supper

NAT TURNER reappears
DEEP in WOODS,
this time tho'
MUTHA WIT has Followed.
AS
HAMMET pats RON's Face trying to Wake him.
HAMMET Begins to Kiss.
BUT
RON: don't. uh. don't do that.

HAMMET: you don't lak it?

RON: no uh yes. i like it. it's just—

HAMMET: i lak you.

NAT *(to GOD)*: where's ham?

(silence.)

last time I was heah I wasn't feelin' too good

HAMMET: i was ready my mind was but

NAT: but my body it said

RON: wait.

listen to me

. . . you scared . . . ? . . .

HAMMET: . . . a little bit

a little bit . . .

RON: don't go then. don't go tonight.

HAMMET: Gotta.

RON: You don't gotta—

HAMMET: Gotta.

Be Free.

NAT: Where. Ham?

RON: you ready to Die?

HAMMET & NAT: mind body

feet soul

say Go

RON: Go where?!

NAT: JERUSALEM!!!

RON: you'll never make it there!

NAT: it's closer than they think

HAMMET: we gon have lotsa folks joinin' in I know

NAT: mark my words

HAMMET: you ain't gat somethin' ta die fo'?

where you come from

you ain't gat somethin' you willin'

ta die fo'?

. . . huh? . . . ? . . .

RON: No . . .

HAMMET: I do.
RON: where I come from
   if you die
   it's over
   if you die they win
   you cain't fight no more
   if you're dead
   it's over.
NAT: he rose.
HAMMET: i'm willin' ta die
NAT: after that dinner
   he went out there
   walked among the trees
HAMMET: i'm willin' to kill
NAT: climbed that hill
   wit that wood on his back
   they nailed 'im up
HAMMET: fo' freedom
NAT: three days later
   He ROSE.
RON: you're scared.
NAT: a little
HAMMET: I'm scared . . .
NAT: a little bit
HAMMET: Nat say—
NAT & HAMMET: Gawds wit us.
HAMMET: He on oura side
   backin' us up
   can't nobody take that from us
   can't no bullets
   no whips
   no chains
   no
   nuthin
   cain't nobody take that from us
   . . . backin' us up
   he backin' us up

(NAT breaks BREAD and drinks WINE)

blood don't scare me it scare you?
RON: yes! and it should scare you a whole lot.
HAMMET: I know blood
    I know dat
    I kill somebody
    there's blood then they die
    chop 'im stab 'im cut 'im beat 'im
    Blood
    Dead
    I know that
    dat don't scare me none
    but
* NAT: before they nailed 'im ta that cross
    befo'
    at that last suppa
    he say
    his right-hand man
    his buddy
    gon give 'im up
    he say ta his buddy's face
    "one o' y'all gon give me up"
    . . . Where. Ham.
* HAMMET: . . . how long
    . . . how far
    . . . how many
    . . . don't. know.

(NAT quickly Exits.
MUTHA WIT watches RON and HAMMET.)

unknown
a li'l bit
dat scare me a li'l bit
. . . you wanna com?

            you can if you want ta
            even if you scared
            I'll protect ya
            you wanna
            you wanna com?
RON: no.
            I'm not willing
            . . .
            to kill to stab to cut to beat—
HAMMET: it's okay to be scared
RON: it's not just that!
HAMMET: I'll protect you
RON: No!
            you don't get it I can't fight!
            . . .
            I don't know how
            I don't know how to
            fight
            I mean really
            really
            fight
            take another life
            I could never
            do something like that I
            I cain't
            NO
            No
            no
HAMMET: . . . okay.
RON: . . . sorry . . .
HAMMET: okay . . .
            you free anyway . . .
RON: huh?
HAMMET: . . . you a free nigga ain't ya?
RON: . . . yeah.
            I'm free.
HAMMET: How dat feel?

You can walk where and when ya wanta cain't ya do
whateva com' ta mind when it com' ta mind—
how dat feel?

(RON HAS NO ANSWER.)

... i don't know what i'ma do when i'm free lak ya'self probably just jump. you know? when i gits freedom i'm gon'
jump. you won't be able to even keep me on the ground
people com' by look at me lak i'm crazy "what you jumpin'
fo' hammet com' on back down heah boy" i'm just gon'
jump. jump till i touch the sky. these hands. they small i
know but they ready. these feet. they quick. you probably
can't understand bein' free n' all but that's okay. you a
funny guy you know that i lak you you funny not many people stand up ta ova seea jones n' nat turner in the same day
lak you that one reason i lak you. i think you wrong tho'
you can fight from what i seen i think you wrong on that.

(THEY Watch Each Other.
HAMMET moves Closer to RON.
HAMMET Touches RON'S Face.
They KISS.
Quiet.)

RON: I don't even know your name.
HAMMET: My name is Ham.
    Hammet.
RON: Hammet.
    Hammet.
    no one's going to believe this Hammet
    only in my dreams only in my wildest dreams
    I could only be makin' this up—

(They KISS once more.)

HAMMET: how dat feel.
RON: ... nice.

(beat.
they smile.
beat.
HAMMET takes RON into his ARMS.)

HAMMET: you ain't gat no special somebody?
one you say anythang to
do anythang wit
makes ya glow
when you heah the name?
RON: . . . no.
HAMMET: i be yo' somebody . . . if ya want.

(RON Begins To Answer Him.)

blow me.
RON: . . . what?
HAMMET: blow me
fill me
wit you

(HAMMET opens his mouth.
RON realizes what he's being asked and proceeds to Blow Sweet
Air into HAMMET's mouth.
silence.)

RON: you asked
what it feels like
to be free . . .
lost
i feel lost
sometimes
without a connection
without linkage
without a
past
. . . story . . .
but now—

(T.J. RACES into the SHACK.)

T.J.: they. started. keep. low.
    i can feel myself gittin weaker ronnie
    take my hand
    it's time

(T.J. looks to RON
RON looks to HAMMET
HAMMET looks to RON)

RON: gramps . . .
    . . . i think i might wanna stick around

(the ENTIRE CAST Steps Out of Character And Appears)

OMNES: **YOU THINK YOU MIGHT WANNA STICK AROUND?!!**

(beat.
The CAST turns to Audience.)

    can you believe this fool—
    he wanna stay heah?
    somebody git this man off the stage
    he talkin' 'bout stayin' in Slavery times
    is there a Doctor in the House—
    i'm ready ta git outta these rags—
    check his temperature—
    you gon' up and make me miss my bus—
RON: you people don't understand!!
    We BLEW Each Other.

(DEAD SILENCE.)

    no . . . uh . . . i mean . . .
    he . . .
    he filled me

wit him
and I
I filled him
wit me

(pause.
T.J. Drops. WEAK.
AS
MUTHA WIT appears with Wheelchair
The CAST Retreats into a TABLEAU:
MISTRESS MO'TEL IS BEING HELD DOWN BY NAT
AND BUCK NAKED.
KATIE LYNN STANDS BY HOLDING A WHITE BABY
(WRETCHED JR.)
HAMMET AND IZZIE MAE
WATCH)

gramps are you okay?
T.J.: you cain't stay
you cain't stay heah it ain't possible
you don't belong heah
RON: . . . i think i'm in—
T.J.: not Heah! not. Now!

MASSACRE MOuRN

T.J. SLOWLY CLOSES HIS EYES.
RON STARES IN HORROR.
EVERY NOW AND THEN THE EARTH SHAKES.
SUDDENLY,
MUTHA WIT MOTIONS.
THE TABLEAU MOVES.

MISTRESS MO'TEL: AHHH!!!

> Katie!
>
> Katie Lynn! Katie Lynn! i ain't neva touched a hair on yo' head never beat you never had you beat never laid a hand o' finger on you tell 'em Katie JESUS JESUS Katie Lynn please tell 'em by the grace of Gawd I'm beggin' you don't let them hurt me Katie don't let them hurt Wretched Jr. please Katie Lynn tell 'em we been good ta ya we always treat oura house niggas proper nice and gentle KATIE My Baby my baby boy Wretched Jr. don't take his mama from 'im i'm the only thang he gat left don't let 'em take his mama from 'im KATIE PLEASE PLEASE KATIE LYNN tell 'em!

KATIE LYNN: . . . no. you neva touched me

> you neva beat me
>
> neva slapped me even
>
> you neva don' none of 'em thangs ta me Mistress Mo'tel you just sold Fannie and Pinkey off befo' i gat a chance ta see 'em good you just saw yo' husband sneak outta yo' bed and inta mine nite after nite never sayin' a word ta 'im o' ta me you just worked my mama and papa on this farm 'til they dropped dead and 'xpected me ta do the same naw you never touched me Mistress Mo'tel
>
> not a hair on my nappy head
>
> there i tol' it
>
> nah cut this bitch's head off befo' i do it myself

(NAT proceeds to Decapitate MISTRESS MO'TEL.
KATIE LYNN Hides the Baby's Face.)

> Shh.
>
> Shh.
>
> Wretched Jr.
>
> you fine.
>
> you fine wit me.
>
> wit katie lynn you fine.
>
> Shh.
>
> Shh.

(NAT looks to KATIE LYNN.
KATIE LYNN refuses to give over the Baby.
NAT tries to take WRETCHED JR. away from KATIE LYNN
They Begin a Life and Death Struggle over the Baby.
Finally,
NAT Pins KATIE LYNN down and Motions for HAMMET to
take WHITE BABY from her.
beat.
HAMMET Crosses to Them.
HAMMET snatches Baby
AS
KATIE LYNN's screams are Muffled by NAT's hands.
HAMMET stares at WRETCHED JR.
IZZIE MAE Races toward HAMMET
BUT
BUCK NAKED CATCHES HOLD OF HER.
HAMMET
pauses.
then
HAMMET BEGINS TO RIP THE BABY APART.
IZZIE MAE MELTS.
KATIE LYNN ERUPTS)

KATIE LYNN: NOOOOOOO!!!!

(slight. sound. of. dogs. is. heard)

THIS ONE WAS MINE!!!!
HE TOOK IT!!!!
HE GAVE IT TA HER!!!
THIS ONE WAS MINE HAMMET!!!
THIS WAS MINE!!!

(HAMMET Stunned, Drops the Remains of the Baby.
NAT swiftly drags KATIE LYNN from the SCENE.
BUCK NAKED and IZZIE MAE Quickly Follow.
sounds. of. DOGS. advances.
HAMMET remains.
transfixed on the

> *remains. of. WRETCHED JR.*
> *the. DOGS. are. now. Extremely. CLOSE.*
> *MUTHA WIT Touches T.J. and*
> *INSTANTLY MUTHA WIT, T.J. and RON Begin to RISE*
> *into the AIR*
> *HAMMET begins to CHANT*
> *AS*
> *HE gathers the remains.)*

HAMMET: first.

RON *(Floating)*: run

HAMMET: last.

RON: run hammet.

HAMMET: last.

RON: hammet.

HAMMET: first.

RON: RUN. HAMMET. RUN.

> *(DOGS GATHER OFFSTAGE.*
> *T.J. with Every Ounce of His Strength*
> *grabs hold of RON)*

T.J.: you mine.

> my responsibility was ta bring you heah let you learn take
> you back you wont live heah they'll kill you along wit the
> rest you know you read it you studied it thousands of white
> troops hundreds of dead slaves they'll destroy this place
> History
> HIStory
> cain't be stopped
> do what you can in yo' Own Time
> i need you to LIVE
> Go Back.
> Don't die.
> Don't . . .
> die . . .
> heah . . .
> i. wait. ed. one. hun. dred. year. you. came. birth. life.

shine. i. wait. ed. die. heah. don't. cain't. not. live. not. heah. don't. die. heah. i. knew. much. good. win. we. win. won. you. mine. you. mine. mi. proof. you. mine . . . PROOF.

(T.J. Dies
silence.
THE DOGS ATTACK HAMMET.
snatching his Eyes from the scene
RON takes the dead T.J. into his ARMS.
the entire scene transforms BACK into
THE MOTEL
GERTHA AND OCTAVIA Appear.
In MOTEL Room.
above them
THEY See RON and T.J.
floating.)

GERTHA & OCTAVIA *(Joy)*: ROOONNN . . . RON . . . RON-
NIE . . . RON!!!

(RON watches Them as he Lands
BACK
the family
of the dead
EX-SLAVE
gathers Ron and T.J. in their
ARMS)

RON: holding history
i'm holding history in my arms

(MUTHA WIT MOTIONS THE
WORLD
TO FADE.)

the
BEGINNING

Robert O'Hara received his Directing MFA from Columbia University School of the ARTS in 1996, where he wrote and directed *Insurrection: Holding History* as his Graduate Thesis and staged the World-Premiere Production of *Insurrection: Holding History* at The Joseph Papp Public Theater/New York Shakespeare Festival in November 1996, after serving as a 1995–96 Artist in Residence at the Public Theater, during which time he served as Asst. to the Director of *Bring in 'da Noise/Bring in 'da Funk* and *Blade to the Heat*, both directed by George C. Wolfe. A 1995 Van Lier Fellow at New Dramatists, he is the recipient of Mark Taper Forum's Sherwood Award, the John Golden Award, *Newsday*'s 1996 Oppenheimer Award for Best New American Play, and the 1996 NEA/TCG Theatre Residency Program for Playwrights with American Conservatory Theater. Robert is currently working on several projects for both the Stage and Screen.